Fearless and Free

The National Endowment for the Humanities

1100 Pennsylvania Ave NW

Washington DC 20506

www.neh.gov

Published 2005

ISBN 0-16-072556-9

Fearless and Free

Celebrating the 40th Anniversary of the National Endowment for the Humanities

Ida Proper, watercolor by Jamie Wyeth, courtesy of the artist and the President's Committee on the Arts and the Humanities.

About the Book

This book is adapted from eighteen conversations conducted by
the Chairman of the National Endowment for the Humanities,
Bruce Cole. They first appeared in the pages of *Humanities,* the
Endowment's bimonthly magazine.

About NEH

Founded in 1965, the National Endowment for the Humanities is
an independent grant-making agency of the United States government
dedicated to supporting research, education, preservation, and public
programs in the humanities.

About the Chairman

Bruce Cole became the eighth Chairman of the National Endowment
for the Humanities in December 2001. A scholar of Renaissance
art, he has written fourteen books, including *The Informed Eye:
Understanding Masterpieces of Western Art; The Renaissance Artist at
Work; Titian and Venetian Art, 1450-1590;* and *Sienese Painting in the
Age of the Renaissance.* Cole taught art history and comparative
literature at Indiana University before joining the Endowment.
He earned his M.A. from Oberlin College and his Ph.D. from
Bryn Mawr College.

Introduction

Bruce Cole
Chairman of the National Endowment for the Humanities

The National Endowment for the Humanities marks its fortieth anniversary this year with a look not just at our history but at the challenges of today and tomorrow. In the pages that follow, eighteen thoughtful and fascinating people—among them an historian, a poet, a university professor, a classicist, a critic, a cabinet secretary, an antiques dealer, and a chef—speak to the breadth and vitality of the humanities in this difficult, dangerous era.

The NEH was founded in the belief that cultivating the best of the humanities has tangible benefits for civic life. The words of our founding legislation say that "democracy demands wisdom and vision." Government of, by, and for the people needs educated and thoughtful citizens.

Today we find ourselves in a conflict driven by religion, philosophy, political ideology, and competing views of history—all humanities subjects. Without a continually deeper knowledge of each, we would have no bearings, no sense of how the past informs the present, no experience imagining worlds other than our own.

From Homer through *Beowulf* and beyond, people learned their heritage and history through story and song, and they passed those stories and songs to the next generation.

Great civilizations all cultivate memory; in Abraham Lincoln's words the "mystic chords of memory, stretching from every battlefield and patriot grave to every living heart and hearthstone all over this broad land."

For four decades, the Endowment has enhanced Americans' awareness of their own culture and history and other peoples' as well. With NEH support, teams of scholars have created monographs such as *The Cambridge History of China*, the *Encyclopedia of Islam*, and *The Oxford History of the British Empire*. More than one thousand translations have made key cultural texts available to English-language readers, helping them understand historical, philosophical, and religious developments in other parts of the world. And editions of great texts of scientific thought, including key works by Darwin and Galileo and Newton, have enabled students to explore how scientists approached perplexing questions of the universe.

NEH fellowships have been the single largest supporter of scholarly research in the United States, making possible thousands of publications and presentations.

NEH funds have also helped rescue the raw materials of culture on which this research is based. One million brittle books and seventy million pages of decaying newspapers are now on microfilm thanks to the Endowment's help. But preservation is only part of the story. The NEH has also made these materials accessible to a larger audience, funding hundreds of museum exhibitions, library displays, films, and websites.

In partnership with the fifty-six state and territorial councils, the Endowment has carried American audiences from Tutankhamen in ancient Egypt through the time of the Medici and on to the present. The cultural encounters may take place under a chautauqua tent, around the table of a neighborhood book club, or over the airwaves of local radio.

Technology keeps easing the path. The internet portal EDSITEment (edsitement.neh.gov) provides lesson plans for 150 top-rated websites, while digitization has begun to turn every desktop into the sort of archive no emperor ever imagined. It democratizes knowledge and makes it available at the click of a mouse.

This is just the latest advance in learning. In the past forty nears, tens of thousands of teachers have taken a break from their classrooms to study in Endowment seminars and institutes, returning with renewed energy and deeper understanding.

Nothing could be more important. Too often these days, our young people exhibit an alarming lack of historical knowledge. Often they do not know the basic facts, concepts, and ideals that have continued to sustain our country over the last two and a half centuries. Why does it matter? It matters because a democracy is not self-sustaining. Knowledge of its institutions and values must be transmitted between the generations.

No one has expressed this better than Benjamin Franklin. Emerging from the Constitutional Convention, he was asked by a bystander whether the delegates had given the people a republic or a monarchy. He replied, "A republic, madam—if you can keep it."

This need to keep it is especially important today. When hatred of our liberties, democratic values, and freedoms incite murderous attacks, it is essential that we understand just what our liberties are and how we got them. We cannot defend what we cannot define. To address this urgent national need, President Bush in a Rose Garden speech on Constititution Day 2002 launched the NEH's We the People initiative designed to improve the teaching and understanding of American history and culture. With the president's leadership and with support from both sides of the aisle in Congress, we have launched new programs such as the Landmarks of American History Workshops, where teachers study with experts at the very places where history was made—homes, battlefields, and even whole cities. Building on a twenty-year effort to save, catalog, and microfilm nearly seventy million pages of historic newspapers, the NEH is now, in collaboration with the Library of Congress, beginning to digitize millions of pages that will be available to the American public free and forever. This monumental effort, the National Digital Newspaper Program, will provide the first great draft of our history—unfiltered and searchable. We continue to support publication of the Papers of George Washington and other presidential papers projects.

Thousands of libraries around the country are receiving our We the People Bookshelf, sets of high-quality books for students that explore the great issues of our history, such as freedom or courage or becoming an American. We have also instituted a new lecture series on American heroes and an essay contest on the idea of America exploring the concepts and values that hold us together.

The fearless and free exchange of ideas, respect for individual conscience, belief in the power of education—all these values are implicit in the study of the humanities, and all are on display in the pages that follow. In this anniversary celebration, eighteen men and women speak their creative minds, emboldened by learning and liberty, the essential conditions in which the NEH continues to flourish.

Remembering our past

How history shapes a society

Pulitzer Prize-winning author
David McCullough discusses
the pleasures of learning and
the discoveries that have
accompanied his books.

BRUCE COLE: It seems to me that so much of history is about vast, impersonal forces that act on people. Your books are not about that. Your books are about people, their strengths, their flaws, their heroism.

DAVID McCULLOUGH: Well, Barbara Tuchman said, "There's no trick to interesting people in history or children in history." She said, "You can explain it in two words: tell stories." I think that's true if you're writing for somebody who's six years old or somebody who's sixty-five years old.

It's the sense of discovery or rediscovery that keeps me propelled. People ask, "Are you working on a book?" I say, "Yes. That's right." But I really want to say, "No, I'm working in a book. I'm inside it." And I want to be inside the time.

There are so many mistaken views that people have. First of all, you could make the argument that there's no such thing as the past. Nobody lived in the past.

COLE: That's right. They didn't know how it was all going to work out.

McCULLOUGH: They lived in the present. It was their present, not our present, and they didn't know how it's going to come out, and they weren't *just like we are*, because they lived in that very different time. You can't understand them if you don't understand how they perceived reality, and you don't understand that unless you understand the culture. What did they read? What poetry moved them? What music did they listen to? What did they eat? What were they afraid of? What was it like to travel from one place to another then?

COLE: One of the most vivid experiences I've had in that way was taking a couple of years to read all of Pepys's diary.

McCULLOUGH: Wow. That's no small undertaking.

COLE: It took me years. It was bedtime reading. But that is exactly what I found so riveting: the sense of night without any illumination, no telephones, the communication, the hygiene, and the like told in this marvelous prose. It does transport you.

McCULLOUGH: That's one of the reasons I began *John Adams* as I did, with these two lone men on horseback riding through a bleak, cold winter landscape, temperature in the twenties. For all intents and purposes, they're anonymous. They are coming through that winter scene, the snow and the wind, and they're going to ride nearly four hundred miles in that kind of weather, on horseback, to get to the Continental Congress in Philadelphia. These were tough people. We see them in paintings in their frilled shirts and their satin pants and the powdered hair, and they look like fops. They look like softies. Nothing doing. They were tough. And life was tough.

And yes, of course, they were not gods. Particularly talking to college audiences, I say, never, never think of them as gods. They were human beings with all the failings, flaws, and weaknesses that are part of the human condition. They were imperfect. Life was so short, and they knew it could end almost any time.

COLE: Does your training in painting help you?

McCULLOUGH: I expect so, or maybe it's just we've all been so conditioned by movies. I love Dickens. I love the way he sets a scene. He said, in his great admonition to writers, "I want to know what they had for dinner. I want to know how long it took to walk from where to where."

COLE: That's what makes it human.

McCULLOUGH: You get into it almost the way an actor gets into a part. You scratch the supposedly dead past and what you find is life. It starts to come alive in your head, and you pray to God that you can convey that onto the printed page.

COLE: That's wonderful.

McCULLOUGH: There are innumerable writing problems in an extended work. This book on Adams took a little more than six years. You, the writer, change in six years. Life around you changes. Your family changes. They grow up. They move away. You're also learning more about the subject.

COLE: What do you do with those early chapters?

McCULLOUGH: The voice has to stay the same. So you go back and work on them, in a way, as a painter will work all over the whole canvas. I work on the front and the back and the middle all at once. With biography, I think it's best to pick a subject who lives to a ripe old age. Older people tend to relax and speak their minds. They're dropping some of the masks that they've been wearing through much of life. There's a candor.

With Adams, for example, I had a character who was in motion virtually all of his life up until he left the White House in 1801. He was going to go back to Braintree, Massachusetts, and never leave there for twenty-five years, holding no office, having no influence, and how in the world was I going to sustain that?

As it turned out, that's when the inward journey begins for John Adams, and that to me, in many ways, was the most interesting part of the whole book. He begins to realize that many of the things that he has thought or held to for so long he doesn't see as he did before.

The concept, for example, of the Enlightenment, that if one applied the combined intellectual efforts of a good society, there was no answer that couldn't be found. Well, he decided that that really wasn't so, that inevitably there were unsolvable mysteries about life and that it was best that way.

COLE: You bring first-rate scholarship to a wide audience in a way that is both literary and accessible.

McCULLOUGH: Well, thank you. It's what I try very hard to do. I had the advantage of an education in the humanities. Being an English major at Yale in the 1950s was a privilege. People like John O'Hara, John Hersey, Brendan Gill, and Thornton Wilder were around on the campus. There were days when I sat down at the communal lunch table beside Thornton Wilder. There was the daily themes course, which was taught by Robert Penn Warren.

After Yale I served a valuable apprenticeship, first at *Time* and *Life*, then at the U.S. Information Agency, then at *American Heritage*. Once I discovered the endless fascination of doing the research and of doing the writing, I knew I had found what I wanted to do in my life.

Every book is a new journey.

With a book like *John Adams*, I've spent six glorious years in the eighteenth century. To go into that time, it is necessary not just to read what they wrote—*they* meaning John and Abigail Adams and others in their circle—but to try and read what they read. To go back and read Swift and Defoe and Samuel Johnson and Smollett and Pope—all those people we had to read in college English courses—to read them now is to have one of the infinite pleasures in life.

Pick up Samuel Johnson's essays or Francis Parkman's works on the French and Indian War, and it's humbling. But it also is affirming in the sense that you realize that you're working in a great tradition.

COLE: Aside from Parkman who are your heroes?

McCULLOUGH: There are certain books that I like very much. *Reveille in Washington.* I love Barbara Tuchman's work, particularly *The Proud Tower.* Paul Horgan's biography of Archbishop Lamy is a masterpiece. I'm fond of Wallace Stegner's book on John Wesley Powell.

I like some of the present-day people: Robert Caro's first volume on Lyndon Johnson was brilliant. I care for some of the best of the Civil War writing: Shelby Foote, for example, and Bruce Catton's *A Stillness at Appomattox.*

COLE: Do you find the research or the writing harder? I think writing is just an agony. It's a clarifying process. It really shows you where you have to fill in the gaps.

McCULLOUGH: You can target your efforts much more clearly. I love to go to the places where things happen. I like to walk the walk and see how the light falls and what winter feels like. Or look at Carpenters' Hall in Philadelphia. That's a beautiful little Georgian red brick structure, about fifty by fifty. It has all the ideals of the eighteenth century: balance and light. You go in there and you think, "This is where the first Continental Congress met. One of the greatest beginnings in all of history began in this little room?"

COLE: I was amazed about the populations of New York and Boston—how small they were and how big the British army was. That does help put it into perspective.

McCULLOUGH: When I read that the British army had landed thirty-two thousand troops—and I had realized, not very long before, that Philadelphia only had thirty thousand people in it—

it practically lifted me out of my chair. They landed an army bigger than the entire population of the largest city in the country.

COLE: That's an amazing fact. It would be wonderful if there were more historians working in the way that you do. It seems to me that many academic historians are writing more and more for specialized audiences.

McCULLOUGH: I feel I'm working in a tradition that goes all the way back to Thucydides or Gibbon, if you want. They weren't academic historians either.

I don't feel that there is a great divide between the work that I and others do and those in the academic world. There are superb writers who are academic historians: Bernard Bailyn, William Leuchtenburg, Kenneth Jackson.

COLE: A study done not too long ago that surveyed fifty top colleges and universities showed the lack of historical knowledge was really appalling.

McCULLOUGH: I have been lecturing at colleges and universities continuously for twenty-five years or more. From my experience, I don't think there's any question whatsoever that the students in our institutions of higher learning have less grasp of American history than ever before. We are raising a generation of young Americans who are, to a very large degree, historically illiterate.

Our way of life could very well be in jeopardy because of this. Since September 11, it seems to me that never in our lifetime, except possibly in the early stages of World War II, has it been clearer that we have—as a source of strength, a source of direction, a source of inspiration—our story. Yes, this is a dangerous time. Yes, this is a time full of shadows and fear. But we have been through worse before, and we have faced more difficult days before. We have shown courage and determination, and skillful and inventive and courageous and committed responses to crisis before. We should draw on our story; we should draw on our history as we've never drawn before.

COLE: Our strength comes from our story.

McCULLOUGH: Absolutely. If we don't know who we are, if we don't know how we became what we are, we're going to start suffering from all the obvious detrimental effects of amnesia.

What did the Founders mean by "the pursuit of happiness"? They did not mean material wealth. They did not mean ease, luxury.

COLE: Happiness in our sense.

McCULLOUGH: As near as I can tell, they meant the life of the mind and the life of the spirit. John Adams wrote a letter to his boy, John Quincy, concerned that the boy not just be studying Greek and Latin but that he be reading the great works in his own mother tongue, particularly the English poets.

He says, "Read somewhat in the English poets every day. You will find them elegant, entertaining and constructive companions through your whole life." That's when he says this famous line, "You will never be alone with a poet in your pocket."

COLE: That's wonderful.

McCULLOUGH: One of the regrets of my life is that I did not study Latin. I'm absolutely convinced, the more I understand these eighteenth-century people, that it was that grounding in Greek and Latin that gave them their sense of the classic virtues: the classic ideals of honor, virtue, the good society, and their historic examples of what they could try to live up to.

I feel that what I do is a calling, and I would pay to do what I do if I had to. I will never live long enough to do the work I want to do: the books I would like to write, the ideas I would like to explore.

David McCullough is the author of eight books—his first was *The Johnstown Flood* and his most recent is *1776*. He won Pulitzer Prizes for *Truman* and *John Adams*, and National Book Awards for *The Path Between the Seas: The Creation of the Panama Canal, 1870-1914* and *Mornings on Horseback*. He is a National Humanities Medalist and was the 2003 Jefferson Lecturer in the Humanities.

Presidential Papers Projects
supported by NEH include:

Papers of George Washington
University of Virginia

Papers of Thomas Jefferson
Princeton University

Papers of John and
John Quincy Adams
Massachusetts Historical Society

Papers of James Madison
University of Virginia

Papers of Andrew Jackson
University of Tennessee

Correspondence of
James K. Polk
University of Tennessee

Legal Papers of
Abraham Lincoln
Illinois Historic
Preservation Agency

Papers of Andrew Johnson
University of Tennessee

Papers of Ulysses S. Grant
Southern Illinois University

Dwight David Eisenhower Papers
Johns Hopkins University

On the trail of Lewis and Clark

"Successful in spite of their failures"

Editor Gary Moulton relives the adventures through the pages of their journals.

BRUCE COLE: You've lived with Lewis and Clark for twenty years as editor of the journals of their experience. What have you learned from this? Have your ideas about them changed?

GARY MOULTON: One of the things that I learned first was that I wasn't really competent to do this because I'm a historian, and Lewis and Clark were engaged in a great number of scientific inquiries. I found out quickly that I had to find experts to help me.

COLE: Things like botany and geology and —

MOULTON: Botany and linguistics and ethnology and meteorology and astronomical observations and on and on and on—all the sciences they were engaged in. That was a revelation and it challenged me intellectually more than I'd ever been challenged before. Lewis and Clark was not just a trek across the wilderness West—it was an endeavor of scientific proportions as well.

COLE: Let's talk about what resulted from this great voyage of discovery. What contributions did it make in terms of cartography and botany and the understanding of the various languages and the like? Was this a successful expedition?

MOULTON: The phrase I use is that Lewis and Clark were successful in spite of their failures. Some of the things that were set as goals for them by Thomas Jefferson they didn't succeed at. No one could have succeeded because the tasks were unrealistic: that is, find an all-water route and northwest passage to the coast. No such passage existed. The geographical conceptions of the time were that the Rocky Mountains were a low-lying set of hills and that they were connecting streams between the Missouri and the Columbia that were easily portaged; Lewis and Clark disproved all those ideas under the hardest circumstances.

But I think they were successful because they accomplished getting there and back without any great loss of life. Only one member of the party died on the whole trip. Two Indians were killed. In spite of the confrontation with the Blackfeet Indians in Montana, almost all of their meetings with Indians were friendly and helpful and mutually beneficial.

The other things—many of the scientific accomplishments—have been coming to light in just the last twenty or thirty years.

Let me give you an instance of that—their botanical collection. There are more than 240 plants at the Academy of Natural Sciences in Philadelphia. People are taking small pieces of those plants and doing cellular studies to try to get a snapshot of the environmental conditions before industrialization.

That is just one thing. People are also working with the maps and the journals and the Indian tribal materials and the weather data and bringing up all sorts of new studies.

COLE: So this project of discovery still goes on?

MOULTON: Absolutely.

COLE: What about Lewis and Clark themselves? What kind of people were they? They somehow were able to work with a disparate group of people, some of them pretty rough and ready. What was that dynamic like?

MOULTON: They were simply two very different characters and personalities who were able to work together. I don't see how it happened. There were only two or three instances of disagreement, and those were over minor matters. "Do you like salt?" "Do you not like salt?" "Do you like dog meat?" Unimportant things. In terms of sharing the command of the men, there is not a breath of disagreement or antagonism between them.

They shared the duties as well. Lewis was the scientist. He took the astronomical observations. He was the naturalist. Clark was the cartographer. He did the surveying, made the maps. So they had these different personalities, but somehow it worked for them. They were able to overcome any personal desire for self-aggrandizement and go on with their work.

COLE: Do you think there was a moment when they thought that this expedition would fail?

MOULTON: I don't think there ever was. Any sense of foreboding or any negative feelings don't appear in the journals. More often they would write "The men in high spirits. I'm going ahead." "We proceeded on" is a phrase they used in the journals quite often, and I think it adds more than a sense of just forward movement.

COLE: What happened to them after the expedition?

MOULTON: Well, Lewis, as you know, committed suicide in October of 1809, three years after the expedition. Now there are some people who don't accept that. They believe he was murdered. But the evidence all points to suicide. Jefferson accepted suicide, Clark accepted suicide—the two people who knew him best.

Lewis had gone through some very difficult times in those three years. He had been looking for a wife and couldn't find someone to go back to St. Louis with him. He got involved in the fur trade, sort of the dot-com of his day, and was probably overextended financially. He sent some men up the river to take an Indian chief home. They failed, so he hired a larger group and committed federal funds to it. When he sent in the bills on that, some clerk in the War Department just stamped it Reject and sent it back. In his day you were individually responsible for those debts if they were rejected.

Clark, on the other hand, had a very successful career. He was married twice, had several children, was a government official. He didn't die until the 1830s and is buried in St. Louis.

COLE: Let's go back to Jefferson for a minute. When did this idea hatch in Jefferson's mind? What did he expect and were his expectations met?

MOULTON: Jefferson's ideas about western exploration really started twenty years before Lewis and Clark. He had tried to send out at least four other groups to explore the West, but, either from one misstep or another, it was never accomplished.

In 1802 he read an account by a Canadian explorer named Alexander MacKenzie, who was working for the Hudson's

Bay Company, and made a trek across the continent. It was a challenge to the United States.

COLE: Kind of like Sputnik?

MOULTON: That's right. And like Kennedy, he said, "We've got to do something." He marshaled all his resources to meet that challenge and to plant the American flag on the Pacific coast and make a statement about the United States' geopolitical ambitions. He had Lewis there as his private investigator—he had known him for years. He had had this vision, and he wrote out for Lewis a set of instructions that encapsulated all the things he had been planning and dreaming and thinking about for twenty years.

The mission was to go before the Louisiana Purchase was consummated. Then, with the Louisiana Purchase completed, Lewis could be investigating American lands as well as new lands.

COLE: What do we know about Jefferson's reaction to the expedition? Was he satisfied?

MOULTON: I think he was very satisfied. He was in correspondence with scientists all over the world, and he was sending them botanical specimens from the expedition. He was telling them about the discoveries along the Missouri River and to the coast. You can see in his correspondence that he's delighted with the exploration and with the discoveries. I think, though, he was disappointed that Lewis wasn't able to get a report out to the nation and make the world aware of all the discoveries.

COLE: Is there life after Lewis and Clark?

MOULTON: Well, I'm not through with Lewis and Clark. I've just completed an abridged version of the thirteen volumes.

COLE: Let me ask you about editing. What does an editor do in a massive project like this? What is your role?

MOULTON: Editors do two things: first we try to ensure that we have an accurate text. That's first and foremost: multiple readings, careful checking, going back to the original sources,

not being satisfied until we have done everything we possibly can to get a reliable text.

The second part is the explication of the text. We want to make sure that we explain to the readers all the parts of the text that might be unclear or need expanding—that is, who are these Indians that they're calling by this name, what is their modern designation, what is this plant that they discovered?

COLE: As an art historian I want to ask you a few questions about images. One of the things that fascinates me is the Indian Peace Medal. This is an object that comes really right out of the Renaissance. Of course, that was not the first Indian Peace Medal; is that right?

MOULTON: Absolutely. It began with Washington's administration and goes back to a European tradition. Lewis and Clark took some of the Washington medals with them. They had different grades and sizes—some for chiefs, some for headmen, some for more prominent persons. The Jefferson Peace Medal was the one that they reserved for the most prominent people.

COLE: Clark brought along a slave, York.

MOULTON: Yes.

COLE: What was their relationship during this expedition? Did that change when they returned?

MOULTON: The traditional view of Clark's relationship with York has been that it was a paternalistic, almost brotherly relationship. They were about the same age. Clark had received York as an inheritance from his father.

On the expedition, York had experiences that were very different from those of Virginia slaves as a whole. He was allowed to carry a rifle and to hunt, and Virginia slaves were not allowed to have weapons. Moreover, on one occasion when they took a vote on where to stay, York's vote is recorded also. This is always seen as significant.

After the expedition, this changed considerably. We only know this because in the last few years a stash of letters from Clark to his older brother have been discovered, and there's quite a bit about York in this newly discovered material. It shows that Clark was rather a harsh slave master. He beat York on a number of occasions.

COLE: What was the previous scholarship on Lewis and Clark?

MOULTON: A sergeant on the expedition had his journals published even before Lewis and Clark got theirs out. The first fully edited, annotated edition came out at the centennial of the expedition, 1904-05.

As new manuscripts were discovered over the years, they in turn were published. By the late seventies the desire was to bring all these things together in one comprehensive whole. That's what spurred the University of Nebraska Press and the Center for Great Plains Studies to get on it. I can't tell you how much the support of NEH has meant to me over the years.

COLE: The agency has been delighted to help make the journals edition possible. This is a monumental piece of scholarship that I point to with pride.

Gary Moulton spent twenty years editing the journals of Lewis and Clark. In addition to the thirteen-volume *The Definitive Journals of the Lewis and Clark Expedition*, his published works include a one-volume abridgment of the *Journals* and *John Ross, Cherokee Chief*. He is the Thomas C. Sorenson Professor of American History at the University of Nebraska at Lincoln.

The Definitive Journals of the Lewis and Clark Expedition, edited by Gary Moulton fill thirteen volumes.

The exhibition "Lewis and Clark in Indian Country" looks at five Native American tribes that the explorers encountered on their journey to the Pacific Ocean.

In 2003, the Great Plains Chautauqua marked the bicentennial of the Lewis and Clark expedition with From Sea to Shining Sea, a program that included portrayals of William Clark, York, Tecumseh, Sacagawea, and John Jacob Astor.

More than 115,000 people viewed the exhibition "Sacred Encounters: Father DeSmet and the Indians of the Rocky Mountain West" at the Museum of the Rockies in Bozeman, Montana.

Filmmakers Ken Burns and Stephen Ives explore the many facets of America's westward expansion in *The West*.

By cataloging and digitizing 50,000 historic photographs, the Denver Public Library has preserved vestiges of the old West.

California's Oakland Museum's "Gold Fever!" exhibition kicked off a three-year commemoration of the gold rush and attracted 190,000 visitors.

Web de Anza, (anza.uoregon.edu) features documents and multimedia resources related to Captain Juan Bautista de Anza's two overland expeditions to northern California from 1774 to1776.

The High Desert Museum in Bend, Oregon, explored the lives of Chinese immigrants during the gold rush in the exhibition "Gum San: Land of the Golden Mountain."

With support from NEH and state humanities councils, the exhibition "Amerikanuak: Basques in the High Desert" traveled through four states.

Uncovering sunken treasure

A cornfield in Kansas yields a clue to the past

The Hawley brothers
tell about their adventure
with the lost steamship *Arabia*.

BRUCE COLE: You found the steamship *Arabia* full of treasure in a cornfield?

DAVID HAWLEY: In Kansas. A weird place to find it, a buried, sunken shipwreck, in Kansas.

COLE: How did that happen?

DH: Well, the *Arabia* was on its way, as many steamships were back in the 1850s, bringing supplies and passengers to the frontier. The *Arabia* carried 222 tons of freight, and, on this trip, 130 passengers to sixteen towns west of Kansas City. About six or eight miles past Kansas City, it hit a tree. The tree poked a hole in the boat, and it sank. The passengers survived. Cargo and freight did not. It sank in the mud and was buried by the sediment that was deposited on it by the river. Over the years, the river changed its course, and we found it a half mile from the present course, buried forty-five feet under a Kansas farm field.

COLE: How did you know where to look?

DH: We read an old newspaper printed at the time. It sank on September 5, 1856. The newspaper said that it sank a mile below a town called Parkville. Parkville is still there today. I bought an old map, and I drew the old map onto a new map to see where the river channel had once been. I put a circle on the map and just walked back and forth up and down the cornrows with a metal detector and found the boilers and engines.

COLE: So you started off as treasure hunters?

GREG HAWLEY: Absolutely. We're three refrigeration repairmen, a restaurant owner, and a guy who digs sewer-line ditches, and that's us.

COLE: That's a great part of the story, though—that you all did it on your own. You found it, and you financed it yourselves. The *Arabia* was said to carry four hundred barrels of Kentucky's finest bourbon whiskey. Was that the fascination, the liquid treasure? What else were you looking for?

DH: I don't think we really thought we'd find a box of gold. It was more the adventure of going out and looking for it. Our budget was fifty or sixty thousand dollars. We thought we would find at least that much of value.

COLE: What did people think about this?

DH: Well, I don't remember talking a whole lot about it. Friends kind of knew. And when we'd go out looking for equipment—pumps and screen wire and stuff—it would come up in the conversation. There was certainly an air of skepticism, but most of the guys we talked to thought, wow, that does sound like fun.

GH: A project that was going to cost sixty thousand dollars in 1985 ballooned to a two hundred fifty thousand dollar budget in 1988, when we broke ground. That was a huge amount of money to us. It was supposed to last the entire dig and we spent it all in three-and-a-half weeks.

So there were a lot of people out there who were our friends who didn't tell us we were nuts, and yet behind the scenes I think they were saying, "Boy, these Hawleys are in really big trouble."

COLE: One of the things I've learned from your museum is that there are all sorts of sunken ships in the Missouri or the Missouri's old course. This was something like your fifth or sixth choice of boats, the *Arabia*? Before you decided on this boat, what kind of research did you do?

DH: Through old newspapers, primarily. One of the greatest frustrations is that the newspaper accounts of steamboat wrecks are very brief. You'll find out more about what happened at the county fair and who won the blueberry pie contest.

COLE: Because it's a common occurrence, for one thing?

DH: Yes. We thought perhaps in the National Archives in Washington there would be more information. And there was,

but I found that it's best to do your local research locally. We gathered as much information as we could about the boat, which wasn't reams and reams. We did find the names of all the merchants, the towns that they were in, the numbers of boxes that they lost.

COLE: How did you find that?

DH: That was in a St. Louis newspaper. A clerk from the ship must have had the list upstairs in his office, and when it sank he had time to gather it up. He carried it back to St. Louis, and he reported it to the newspaper. He gave the name of the towns, the names of the merchants, and the amount of cargo lost but not what was in each box

GH: In the case of the *Arabia*, the cargo was insured for ten thousand dollars. Not much today, but back then, when people made five cents an hour, that was a lot of money. As you begin to do your research and you're trying to figure out which boat you want to choose, eight, ten, fifteen thousand dollars is about the high end on these vessels.

And the farmer was a good guy. One landowner said he wanted 80 percent of what the things brought at auction. This farmer wanted only 15 percent of the proceeds. And when we decided later that we were going to create a museum with our portion, he was even more generous. He asked for just twenty-five items to give his children and grandchildren, and he gave the rest to us. He took no one-of-a-kinds, nothing that would break up a set. We've long felt that we dug a good boat from the best landowner on this river.

COLE: Tell us about the boat. Where was she built, what did she look like?

DH: It was built in Brownsville, Pennsylvania, in 1853 at Pringle's Shipyard. They made about twenty-four boats a year. It came down the Monongahela River to the Ohio. It traveled down the Ohio to the Mississippi and traveled on the Mississippi River from New Orleans to St. Louis until 1855. Then, under new owners, it came on the Missouri River and traveled here until it sank on September 5, 1856. It was just three years old when it sank.

COLE: Which you say is not unusual.

GH: Yes. Of the four hundred boats estimated to have sunk—two hundred and eighty-nine documented—70 percent of them are thought to have been sunk by tree snags, the other 30 percent by fires, high winds blowing them into bridges, boiler explosions, or just taken apart and used to rebuild other boats.

DH: When the Missouri River wanted to move, it didn't matter if a tree was there or not. It would undercut those trees, and they would wash into the river. The roots would get stuck in the bottom of the river and the current of the river would swing this tree facing downstream. Then, over the years, it would shave off the small branches and rot the tree off at water level.

COLE: So it was like a spear?

DH: Yes, with the roots tight in the bottom of the river. You couldn't see them. That's what took them down.

COLE: What was she carrying?

DH: St. Louis was sort of the distribution hub of the Midwest then. Freight was brought to St. Louis from all over the world up the Mississippi River and on rail lines. That was one of the fascinating things, I thought, about the boat. Even back in the 1850s, international trade was very well developed. We found silk that came from the Orient and dishes from England and tobacco from South America and perfume from France.

COLE: You find out a lot about what's going on with trade when you find this kind of cargo.

GH: Now be mindful, the boat sank before Abraham Lincoln was president. It sank before the Civil War. We reached the boat, we uncovered the left paddle wheel and lying in the spokes of the wheel is our first artifact. It's a little bitty shoe. We washed it off, and it's a rubber shoe with the word Goodyear stamped on the sole, with a patent date of 1849.

COLE: There were some pretty fancy goods on this ship. Champagne and brandy, right? And some nice clothes.

DH: Gold-trimmed dishes.

GH: Pots and pans with nonstick cooking surfaces. Our perception of pioneer life changed dramatically during this dig. The emphasis began to switch from the monetary to the historical.

COLE: And you got interested, then, in preservation and the whole network of historical connections and life?

DH: Yes.

COLE: When was the last time somebody could see this boat before it was completely covered up with silt?

DH: Eighteen sixty-six. There was low water in the winter. It was reported in the newspaper that they saw the upper workings of the boat, probably the paddle wheel. Then in 1897, they drilled down to the deck in a big steel tube.

COLE: Tell us about your own excavation.

GH: In some ways, we had some benefits because we researched how other people tried. The first two attempts used coffer dams to try to hold back the mud and water. But there is more water running below the sand than there is running in the river. It doesn't run as quickly, but the volume is much greater. Trying to dig a hole in that is like trying to dig a ditch through quicksand.

So my dad, who is an extraordinarily brilliant guy, came up with the idea of circling the *Arabia* using irrigation wells. Irrigation wells have pumps clear to bedrock, sixty-five feet down, and you can push water a great distance.

So we basically pushed the water from the earth. Our fuel bill went out of sight, but with twenty wells pumping twenty thousand gallons a minute, twenty-four hours a day, we finally lowered the water table below this boat and began to salvage this vessel.

We dug the *Arabia* in four-and-a-half months, which gives most archaeologists aneurysms. But what was apparent to us is that when we finally did lower the water table, we introduced oxygen into what had been an anaerobic environment all these years. We, of course, had an archaeologist, but we had to always ride that fence between slowing down for documentation and speeding up for the sake of the collection.

DH: In addition to that, we were in a flood plain. If the rains were to come, it would wash the dig out. It could have been a wet spring. So we had to be out by then.

COLE: You got the water out. You started digging. What was it like when you first saw something?

DH: We found so many things that someone said, "Every day was like Christmas." And it was.

My favorite things were the pie fillings that we found. I love photography. I took pictures of those and got them back from the lab and realized this colored photograph of this blueberry is the only colored photograph like that in the world—cameras back then were all black and white.

The boat almost became this portal into the past where you could go back to Abraham Lincoln's time and gather up an armful of stuff and bring it back into today's world and see it and smell it and taste it.

COLE: Greg, what was your favorite thing?

GH: When you found somebody's personal luggage, for me and I think for others, that was our great discovery. When you lifted the lid on a personal box, without saying anything, it almost turned into a reverent experience. You were invading someone's life. You didn't feel like you should be there and yet it was okay.

When you lifted the lid, you could tell if it was a male or a female traveler. You could tell if they were wealthy or poor. You could tell if they had children, if there were toys. You could tell by the items if they were tall or short from the size of their pants or the size of their shoes. Whether they were male or female or rich or poor, you saw what they held most precious, what they chose above all else in their life to move west.

COLE: So those are the kinds of moments that turned your efforts from being treasure hunters to being preservationists and wanting to keep this together?

DH: Exactly. When you realized the real wealth of this collection was not in selling it to somebody—it's keeping it together—that sets a whole new course. We had to begin to learn about preservation. And we needed a big building.

All that had to be figured out rather quickly when preservation became an issue. We had read in books that when they'd find prehistoric animals buried in ice, they were still in pretty good shape. So we decided let's freeze things.

Then we thought, "We'll try and trick these artifacts into thinking they are still in the ground. We'll lease an underground storage area, we'll buy galvanized stock tanks, fill them with water, and we'll put some of the artifacts in water." We would work all day and then from eight o'clock at night, when we got back to town, until midnight is when we would clean these things.

GH: Stabilize them.

DH: Some went to the freezers and some went to the coolers and some things, like iron and bricks, were just stored and dried in temperature-controlled rooms. That was the last thing we would do each day.

GH: As we started tracking down conservators, their questions were, well, what in the world are you doing with this stuff? You just can't bring things out of the ground, two hundred tons of artifacts, and then decide you're going to be conservators.

Being in the refrigeration business, controlling humidity and temperature is what we've always done. Then our partner, Jerry Mackey, who owned a hamburger restaurant, gave us a temporary solution. He had huge walk-in freezers and coolers. So we were pushing tenderloins to one side, and we were putting kegs of butter and cheese and lard and soap on the other side. The health department about had a fit. But they were so enthralled, they let us do this.

Once we had the cargo stable, we could begin to be more methodical in our approach to tracking down the right conservators. One of the things that was surprising to us— here we lived in this wonderful country with all this great technology, and yet as a nation we don't dedicate a lot of dollars to historical preservation, not like the Europeans and the Canadians do. Our search went beyond the borders of this country and into the European countries.

Mark Jones, who was one of the chief conservators with Britain's *Mary Rose* Trust, said, "Well, how come you're calling clear over here and you're not talking with the Canadian Conservation Institute?" I didn't even know there was such a thing.

We called them up. A great, great institution. They provided workshops and were willing to take guys like us under their wing. They introduced us to freeze-drying and the different archival lacquers, waxes, and polymers that one needs, and we began to experiment on scraps of wood, leather, textiles. As we began to understand and have success with these small pieces of items, we began to move to the main collection.

COLE: You have this huge collection. You could have auctioned it off at that point.

DH: Yes. We just couldn't do it. The collection would have been broken up and the great treasure that we discovered— the story—would have been lost.

COLE: How did you pick the site for the museum?

DH: We needed a big building, and we needed it cheap. We're not subsidized. We had no money. We spent everything we had at the dig. Our budget there was fifty or sixty thousand dollars, and we ended up spending close to a million, and that was mostly borrowed. We've been paying loans back ever since.

GH: We borrowed another seven hundred fifty thousand dollars to do the museum. We had three museum design firms that showed up unsolicited. The cheapest bid we received was $5.5 million, and we did it for seven hundred fifty thousand. We worked full-time jobs, and at night we would come down here, and we would run wire and do plumbing and build the displays, and we learned to bend Plexiglas. So it's a true family-operated business.

COLE: Now your dad is working at the museum. And your mom runs the gift shop, right?

DH: We're all here, yes. We talk to everybody who comes. Dad or Greg or I will say hello and answer questions.

COLE: Part of your museum tour is to the conservation lab on-site.

GH: It's important for people to understand what is involved— not just digging, not just what's on display but the process and the care necessary. Your appreciation for the effort is greatly influenced when you look at those nine hundred and fifty-five boots and shoes, and you learn that they are all hand stitched, they are soaked in chemicals, they are blocked up and freeze-dried and documented. We only get eighty done a year.

While we began as treasure hunters, we want to make sure that we don't perpetuate people digging up artifacts just to sell them. When they see these artifacts and the work commitment that will follow any excavation, they realize the excavation is the easy part. That was something we didn't understand at the time. This is a really important part—not just to educate but to protect these other boats.

COLE: This is an amazing story.

GH: As amazing as it is, it's the tip of the iceberg. Dave might have found this new boat the *Princess*. We've got some core samples off it. We're pretty excited about it.

COLE: What cornfield is that one in?

GH: Soybeans, actually.

DH: After the Civil War, there was a gold rush to Montana. The *Princess*, among others, was going there—three thousand river miles from St. Louis. It sank east of here, maybe about twenty miles or so. A tree snag took it out. There were no salvage attempts on it that I've ever found. It's been left alone.

We've got a drilling outfit that's ready to start as soon as the soybeans are picked. We didn't have this with the *Arabia*, but they've got cameras with lights on them so we can go down and look inside walls when we drill.

COLE: What was on that ship?

DH: It will be a lot of the same things we have here but also gear for the mining folks—picks and shovels.

GH: Plus, we have whale-oil lamps aboard the *Arabia;* this would have kerosene. Our shoes are all wooden pegged; these shoes would be hobnail and stitching.

The *Princess* is a boat from the 1860s. We have the *Arabia* from the 1850s. And we want to go after a forties boat. We want to get the ball rolling on a museum that has a boat from the twenties, thirties, forties, fifties, and sixties; a boat with trade annuities; a boat with military freight.

As entrepreneurs with our experience and background, we have the ability to dig boats and set up museums that will be self-sustaining, that won't be a burden to the taxpayer. The government will not be digging these boats. They just don't have the efficiency to do it. There is truly a moratorium on this kind of work as it pertains to a state or federal agency. It's going to be up to guys like us.

DH: We want school kids to be the diggers. We want to bring them into the dig site and let them experience the things that we did. There is more to learn than just archaeology. There's math. There's science. You can pull in all the disciplines that kids learn in elementary and high school and beyond. We see a museum created by the community for the community.

GH: By letting these kids get involved, you understand truly the sacrifices of your ancestors. By being involved in history, you're more prone to feel a sense of duty to the country. You're more prone to be better at voting and being proactive in the community. The apathy that America has right now is so destructive. We think we can make a huge difference.

COLE: You both are inspirational. Thank you.

David and Greg Hawley spent childhood summers treasure hunting in abandoned gold mines with their father. In 1985, their attention turned to the story of a sunken steamboat lost before the Civil War on the Missouri River. Excavation of the *Arabia* turned the Hawleys from treasure hunting to conservation and educating. They founded the Steamboat *Arabia* Museum to showcase artifacts from the boat.

The exhibition "A Slave Ship Speaks: The Wreck of the *Henrietta Marie*" explored the wreckage of an English merchant vessel that sank in 1701.

Led by nautical archaeologist George Bass, the excavation of a fifth century B.C.E. Mediterranean shipwreck yielded new information about ancient naval construction and maritime commerce.

"Treasures of Tutankhamen," the first blockbuster museum exhibition, drew more than one million visitors in 1978 and 1979.

Scholars at the University of Notre Dame published the main corpus of the Dead Sea Scrolls in sixteen volumes. The deteriorating manuscripts are being digitized by the Ancient Biblical Manuscript Center.

The excavation of the Sanctuary of Poseidon on the Isthmus of Corinth uncovered new details about ancient Greek festival customs.

The little-known story of a cultural crossroads was presented in the exhibition "Antioch: The Lost Ancient City."

The exhibition "Pharaohs of the Sun: Akhenaten, Nefertiti, Tutankhamen" featured artifacts from the abandoned, monotheistic city of Amarna.

Ken Burns's *Baseball*, a nine-part documentary series seen by 43 million viewers during its television premiere, examines the history and personalities of America's national pastime.

UC-Berkeley's Bancroft Library is compiling and publishing the letters, notebooks, and personal documents of writer and humorist Mark Twain.

The *Dictionary of American Regional English* uses letters, diaries, newspapers, and audio recordings to document regional dialects.

Chautauqua brings America's great statesmen, entrepreneurs, and thinkers onstage through scholar-performers. In 2003, the state humanities councils sponsored nearly 7,000 chautauquas in small towns across the country.

The documentary *Born to Trouble: The Adventures of Huckleberry Finn* explores the historical controversy about Twain's famous novel.

"Barn Again," a traveling exhibition hosted by twenty-six states since 1997, charts the development of rural America through its architecture.

"Colorado River: Moving Waters in the Arid West" examines the legal, social, economic, and environmental history of the river. The exhibition visited twenty-two communities in seven states.

A very different world

History in everyday language

Historian John Lukacs
reflects on World War II
and one of its heroes.

BRUCE COLE: You've written about a variety of subjects: the intellectual history of the past five hundred years, the history of the cold war, the city of Budapest, the rise and fall of Europe, the history of the United States. What draws you to a given topic?

JOHN LUKACS: There's a simple answer to this: whatever interests me. Professionally, sometimes, this is a handicap. Other historians may say, "What is he doing on my turf?" Yet I can only say: whatever interests me.

This goes back to a very different world and to a very different time. As you know, I was born in Hungary. I was interested in history, but it was not until I entered the university that I decided that I was going to get a degree in history, a degree not quite the equivalent of an American Ph.D., but by and large similar. That's how I became a historian.

COLE: As a child you were interested in history?

LUKACS: I started to read novels and literature, I would say, in my early teens. When I look back, I was always interested in the kind of literature that has much history in it.

COLE: I understand. Besides your writing, you've had a long career as a college professor. Is there a relationship between your teaching and your research and writing?

LUKACS: Absolutely. I always wanted to write. Frankly, when I got my first teaching position, I said, "All right. This will enable me to write." I was not interested in moving from college to college up the academic ladder.

If I had been appointed to a large university and had taught graduate students, I don't think I would be as good a writer.

I had to talk to undergraduates about complicated things simply but not superficially. It taught me a great deal about economy of expression.

COLE: Well, that's certainly characteristic of your books: you make complicated events and situations crystal clear. So you find that when you're in the classroom, you need to get to the essence of what you're talking about and present it in a way that is fathomable to an undergraduate?

LUKACS: Yes. I have to use my words carefully, and this is what writing is all about. I have shocked many of my historian colleagues by saying that history consists of words and that the words are not just the packaging of the facts. In our minds the facts do not exist apart from the words with which we express them.

COLE: We really don't know what we know or how we know it until we start to either speak it or write it.

LUKACS: Yes. This goes against the rules in the natural sciences: your expression clarifies your mind.

COLE: It's that whole creative process that is scholarship, I think. Many people in the history profession are working in what I would call silos. They are hyperspecialized, and they are really writing for each other.

LUKACS: The bad thing is that often the specialist is not really very much interested in what he's doing. He has picked a specialty because he thinks that this will further him in his profession. The true specialist is an eccentric: he is someone who is really and deeply interested in something about which he wants to know more and more.

There are all kinds of minuscule privileges that come in academic life. Nobody is immune to it. But if the entire emphasis is directed there, that is a deep loss.

COLE: How does your work reflect you?

LUKACS: As I said, whatever I've written or I'm writing about is something that interests me very much. Another thing is that I am constantly aware of the inevitable relationship of history and literature. History is scientific in a way, but it is an art in

another way, in a different way. History is written, thought, taught, spoken in words of everyday language.

COLE: Let's talk for a minute about history as art. This relation between history and literature, I hope you will agree, is found superbly in Churchill?

LUKACS: Oh, yes. Churchill, as you know, was not a professional historian. There's a great English historian named Veronica Wedgwood, who expressed it right. She said, "History is an art—like all the other sciences."

COLE: One of the things you've written about is the concept of the great man. We see this certainly in your wonderful Churchill books. Is this nowadays a less traveled path for historians?

LUKACS: So it is, but that will pass. I can see that we live in a democratic age, and we have to deal with the lives and the history of large numbers of people. Someone who foresaw this, as he foresaw many things, was the great Tocqueville. Tocqueville has a chapter in the second volume of *Democracy in America,* which asks, "What will be the characteristics of historians in democratic times?" I think that small chapter ought to be pasted above the desk of every historian.

COLE: He says, "The writing of history in the age of democracy will be more difficult than and different from the writing of history in ages ruled by aristocratic minorities."

LUKACS: Exactly. I think of this again and again.

COLE: The NEH is launching a new initiative called We the People, and one of its aspects is that we are establishing a lecture series on heroes and heroism, with the idea that individuals do make a difference and do themselves decisively shape history. With that in mind, let's turn to that remarkable figure, Winston Churchill. How long have you been interested in Churchill?

LUKACS: This goes back to when I lived in Hungary in 1940. I was sixteen or seventeen years old. I have greatly admired him since that time. Then I read his history of the Second World War. It took about another thirty years for this to crystallize into what you might call a professional historian's interest.

COLE: Churchill, as far as historians go, has certainly had his ups and downs. Can you talk about that a little bit?

LUKACS: Arthur Balfour, who was a great speaker but had difficulty in writing, said about Churchill's *The World Crisis*—his multivolume history of the First World War—that Churchill had written an autobiography and called it *The World Crisis*, which is both funny and a bit mean.

COLE: What about Churchill's reputation today?

LUKACS: Churchill's reputation today is very high. I think there are two elements in this. I'm not only speaking of his reputation among historians. Compared to the rather mediocre leadership we have had in the western world since him, he stands out and certainly is a heroic figure in the Second World War. That is rather obvious.

But I think there's another element, too, in the stance he took, adversary as he was not only of Hitler but also of Russian communism. I think after the fall of the Soviet empire it became apparent that, by and large, most people had exaggerated the power and the influence of Soviet Russia. The power and the ability of the Germans in World War II was much greater. The Russians were never close to winning the cold war.

COLE: This makes Churchill's role, especially in those dark days that you talk about, even stronger.

LUKACS: Yes. He did not win the Second World War, but he was the one who didn't lose it. He was a single man in Hitler's path. Hitler knew that. He hated Churchill.

COLE: You speak of Churchill as a visionary.

LUKACS: He had visionary powers that were extraordinary. Bismarck said that a great statesman can see correctly, at best, five years ahead. Churchill beat that.

COLE: Do you think his vision matured as he aged or do you think this was always the case?

LUKACS: I think this was always the case. He says some startlingly prophetic things in his earliest books. Yet I think it matured. He knew a great deal about the world.

COLE: I think of him as one of the great Victorians, although he's a little younger than that. He had an active professional life in government with many, many responsibilities and duties;

still he wrote and wrote and wrote, in the way those great Victorians did. How did he find the time to do all of this?

LUKACS: In the 1920s, he lived very well, but he didn't have much money. He had not married for money at all. Sometime in the 1920s he discovered he could make money writing. But it was not money that made him write. He couldn't help it. He had to write.

COLE: What do you think Churchill thought his place in history was going to be? Do we know that?

LUKACS: I cannot tell you, but I tell you he was quite modest about his ability as a historian. He writes these books that are second to none, and he says, "This is not really history. It's a contribution to history." I don't think this was an artificial modesty. He meant that.

COLE: What about his role as a world figure?

LUKACS: I think he knew what he was doing. He knew not only what he ought to do, he knew what it was that he achieved, and what he could have achieved and could not achieve.

COLE: Did he have his eye on how his actions would influence his place in the world?

LUKACS: I don't think that he was a man very much suffused with vanity. At the very end of the war, VE-Day, when the people in London cheered him to high heaven, he said, "No, it was not due to me. It was due to you."

COLE: You've been writing for a decade now that the modern age is over. What makes you think it's coming to an end?

LUKACS: The modern age was the age when Europe extended its power over other continents. It meant many things: white rule, the power of the state, the idea of schooling, the centrality of the family. It was also the age of the book and the age of money. That is changing. One hundred and seventy-five years ago, Tocqueville saw that something truly new was beginning. Aristocratic minorities had ruled; we were in the aristocratic age, and now the age of democracy is beginning. This was a very slow passage, a coexistence of aristocracies and democracies.

As time went on, the power and the prestige and even the social position of the aristocracies declined, and the power and prestige and the influence of the social democratic structure rose. Now democracy is nearly universal. As Tocqueville also said, this is not a simple theory. People thought the age of democracy would be much simpler than when courtiers ruled, but it is not so. What happens is less rule by the people than rule in the name of the people. The people who are doing the ruling have to be nominated and elected, which of course is very democratic. But the very structure of government and election and the actual representation of the people is very complicated.

COLE: What will be the ideas that define the next era?

LUKACS: I'm not a prophet. I'm only a historian. (Laughter.) The wonderful thing about history is—well, wonderful but also maddening—is that it is unpredictable.

John Lukacs was a history professor at Chestnut Hill College in Pennsylvania for forty-seven years. He is the author of twelve books, including *The Hitler of History, Historical Consciousness, The Passing of the Modern Age, Democracy and Populism: Fear and Hatred,* and *Churchill: Visionary, Statesman, Historian.* Lukacs received the T.S. Eliot Award for Creative Writing.

The Virginia Military Institute is using a challenge grant to endow the John A. Adams '71 Center for Military History and Strategic Analysis.

The New Deal Network, an interactive website for teachers and students (newdeal.feri.org), has archived more than 20,000 historical documents.

One hundred twenty libraries hosted From Rosie to Roosevelt: A Film History of Americans in World War II. The scholar-led program explored the political, social, and culture impact of the war.

Using the testimony of survivors, *The Jews of Shanghai,* a two-part radio program, looks at the experience of the more than 100,000 European Jews who fled to Shanghai to escape Hitler's Third Reich.

The documentary *Eisenhower* follows the life of the general who led the D-Day invasion in World War II and his transition from soldier to statesman.

The film *George Marshall and the American Century* profiles the World War II general who helped rebuild postwar Europe.

As leader of the Free French Forces during World War II, Charles de Gaulle began his rise to the presidency of France. The documentary *De Gaulle and France* considers his legacy.

MacArthur traces on film the career of the general whose vow to return to Bataan in World War II made him a legendary figure.

The film *FDR* drew more than 15.7 million viewers when it was first aired in 1994.

The television series *The Great War and the Shaping of the Twentieth Century* explores how the First World War changed the political, social, and economic fabric of Europe.

"Produce for Victory," a poster exhibition about the home front in World War II, has visited more than 100 communities across the country.

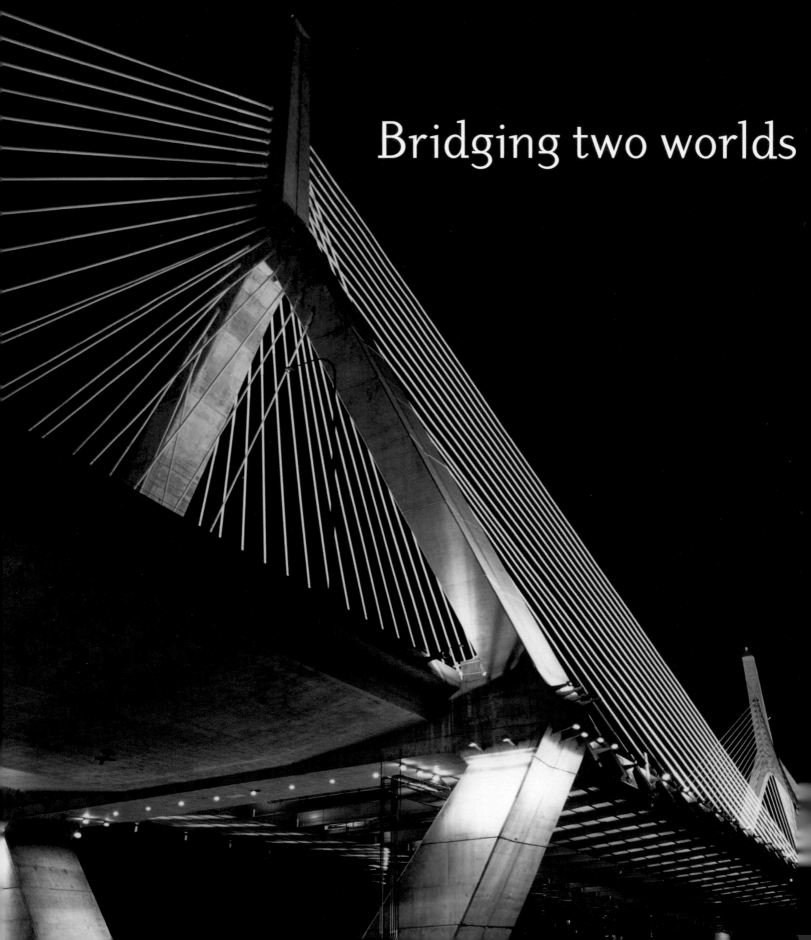

Bridging two worlds

How technology and the humanities are interdependent

Engineer David Billington
finds beauty in structure and
explains the importance of
the humanities to engineers.

BRUCE COLE: You teach a very popular engineering course at Princeton for nonengineers. Why is it important, for humanities students to study engineering and vice versa?

DAVID BILLINGTON: We live in what is often called a technological society. It is important, therefore, that humanities students understand how our society got built and how it functions today. Why engineers should study the humanities is the corollary to that. You can't build the kinds of things we build unless you have a society that is organized in a way that permits and encourages it. Engineering also has a significant influence on the art and literature of its time. We want to make engineers aware of that.

COLE: What led you to the bridging of engineering and the liberal arts?

BILLINGTON: As an undergraduate at Princeton, I took a very strange engineering course called Basic Engineering. It allowed me to take more liberal arts courses than any other engineering program, and it didn't specialize in anything. I took courses in art history, in music, and in literature.

Then I won a Fulbright Scholarship to study in Europe. That was, in a way, my engineering education because I learned structural engineering there. I came back and practiced for eight years and was completely unaware of any kind of tradition that structural engineering at its best would be an art form.

I began to teach in 1960, and because I had worked with architects in practice, I was invited to give a course to architects—graduate students of architecture.

The architects hated what I was teaching. It was all stick diagrams and formulas, and very dry and dull and they despised it. They would bring me pictures of what they considered to be beautiful things—bridges and buildings—and they'd say, "Why can't we study these?" It seemed to me like a reasonable question, but I found nothing in the engineering literature about these things. So with my colleague Robert Mark, who was also confronted with the same questions, I went down to the NEH and got a grant that got us started.

The idea was to study structures that were beautiful and see if they were good engineering. We agreed to split history into two parts. Mark studied things before the Industrial Revolution, and I studied things afterwards.

COLE: What major changes in engineering came out of the Industrial Revolution?

BILLINGTON: The simple answer to that is *everything*. Everything we study now, everything we do in engineering, none of it existed before the Industrial Revolution. Nothing. That's why the Industrial Revolution is the greatest event in modern history.

The two great early innovations were industrialized iron and efficient steam power. There always was iron, and there always was steam power, but they were so inefficient to produce that you couldn't do anything with them.

COLE: Is this true for concrete as well? I'm thinking of the Roman Pantheon.

BILLINGTON: Sure, the Romans had concrete, but they didn't have reinforced concrete. They used concrete in—what we would today call very primitive ways—very clever ways often, but primitive. The Pantheon was built of concrete, but it was very, very heavy, and it cracked substantially.

COLE: Who are some of the great engineering/architecture heroes of the late nineteenth and early twentieth century?

BILLINGTON: Thomas Edison, George Westinghouse, Alexander Graham Bell. These are pretty obvious choices.

COLE: Why did this all happen in the United States? What were the conditions that created this incredible flowering of such innovation?

BILLINGTON: There was a technological infrastructure we got from Britain. In Britain, all over that country, there were little machine shops. Somebody such as James Watt, who was a great inventor and innovator, could connect with John Wilkinson, who was essentially a machinist and knew how to bore cannon and knew how to make, therefore, precise cylinders.

We were suppressed by the British monarchy from having our own industries until the Revolution, but that didn't stop us from having illicit ones and having a lot of technically sophisticated people. When independence came, there was a flowering of this technological infrastructure. Tocqueville, when he came over here, said he couldn't understand it: there was nobody really interested in science, but they had created something that shook the world. He was talking about the steamboat.

COLE: Is there a difference between invention and innovation?

BILLINGTON: Oh, sure, a huge difference. An invention is just an idea that you can show to the patent office as somehow new. An innovation is a new idea that becomes practical.

Edison's electric light system is an example. It's one of the foremost examples of an innovation. Or Bell's telephone is an innovation. Those happen to be inventions as well.

COLE: When you're talking about that practical, seat-of-the-pants idea of innovation isn't Edison a good example?

BILLINGTON: Yes, but I would never call it seat-of-the-pants. This idea that Edison was a tinkerer or the Wright brothers were tinkerers is absolutely wrong. They were first-rate engineers. They operated the way the best engineers always operate—even today. Sure, Edison had to try a lot of things.

Nobody had ever found a solution before for the high-resistance filament. What are you going to use for the filament so it doesn't burn itself up right away? He did have to try and err on a lot of things, but that was all done in a very short period of time. He came to the idea in 1878, and he produced the working lamp in mid- or late 1879.

And he had right next to him one of the best trained mathematical physicists in the country, Francis Upton, who was guiding him in the theoretical sense. He had some of the world's greatest machinists—John Kruesi and some of the others—to build things. Edison ran a research and development operation that was first rate.

Fulton was a first-rate engineer, too. The two of them operated like engineers. That is to say they based their work on calculations, but they also tried things out. They made experiments to make sure that it was going to work. And they read the literature, and they studied what other people had done. They did everything that good engineers do.

COLE: You may not want to speculate on future innovations, but what do you think is next? Are we in a technological revolution with the computer?

BILLINGTON: I don't think so. There's change, but there is nothing at all like the change then. Just imagine the differences between 1780 and 1840.

You had no railroad. You had no telegraph. You even had no steamboat. The difference is monumental. We don't have that kind of change today.

When I was a young man, life was a certain way, with cars and planes and radio and even television. Those are still, today, the major things.

COLE: Let me ask you a little bit about beauty and engineering. When people think about the study of engineering they don't really have beauty in mind. Could you discuss that a bit?

BILLINGTON: Well, based on the stimulus from the architecture graduate students, I began to study, and I went to Europe. I went to Switzerland to see the work of Robert Maillart. Photographs of Maillart's works struck me. They were so striking that I decided to work on Maillart. For the next twenty years I spent my time doing the research that was necessary, to create a written life and works of Maillart and a series of papers and books.

How do you determine beauty? Almost all engineers say, "Oh, well, beauty is in the eye of the beholder" or "That's a relative thing," The only answer that I could find was twofold. One is the sense in which art, real art, becomes classic. People who spend their lives with music don't argue about Mozart and Beethoven and Brahms. There is no longer any argument about them. So I used that classical argument by saying certain works of structure have become classical, such as the Eiffel Tower and Brooklyn Bridge.

COLE: I like your example of the Eiffel Tower, which to me is, in a way, pure engineering, but also one of the most beautiful structures.

I'm thinking particularly about Mies van der Rohe—the idea of how that is exposed by modern architecture.

BILLINGTON: Let me make a sharp distinction between structural art and architecture. Mies van der Rohe was stimulated, as all good architects are, by the culture that surrounded him. Crown Hall is, I would say, an example of a perfectly horrendous structure. It makes no sense whatsoever to a structural engineer, whereas the Hancock Tower in Chicago, which gets the same opprobrium as the Eiffel Tower got, is a work of true structural art. That's because an engineer—Fazlur Khan, one of the great engineers of our story—made the form. There are a few skyscrapers like that. Not many.

COLE: Is this because of the triumph of the architect's aesthetic ideas over good engineering structure?

BILLINGTON: Yes. I'd say it's the feeling that many architects have that engineering structure is simply secondary. They make the form and then they call in the engineer and say, "Make it stand up."

COLE: I'd like to talk more about your work on the Swiss engineer Maillart. You don't think that bridges are architecture? Because, of course, in the history of art, bridges are included.

BILLINGTON: No, sir. They are definitely not architecture. Maillart was not trained as an architect. He didn't practice in architecture. He didn't think like an architect. Those works are works of pure structural art. So it's fine for them to be included in the history of art. That's fine.

COLE: Tell me why bridges are not architecture.

BILLINGTON: Architects are educated to think in terms of space. Architects want to control spaces. Engineers are taught to control forces. Architects are taught to deal with constructions that are going to be intimately used by people.

Engineers are not taught that. Engineers' spaces or engineers' buildings or bridges are used by industry or machines but not intimately by people. Therefore, bridges, except for very small pedestrian bridges, are not essentially built for intimate use by people. The prototypical work of an architect is a private house, and the prototypical work of an engineer is a public bridge.

So bridges and certain kinds of buildings are the work of engineers, whereas schools and churches and office buildings are the work of architects. They use engineers, but the engineers are often secondary.

I don't know if you know the work of Pier Luigi Nervi in Italy or Felix Candela in Mexico. Those are works, buildings, some of them are even churches, where the engineer actually makes the form. They become works of structural art.

Candela built hundreds of things. Some are thin-shell concrete structures. And these are spectacular structures. He was trained as an architect, but he practiced as a builder and a structural engineer. He says that Maillart greatly influenced him. If you ever go to Italy and you look at the Little Sports Palace in Rome, designed by Nervi, you'll see what I mean. I think it's the most spectacular interior space of the twentieth century. And it is designed entirely by an engineer.

David Billington is a professor of civil engineering and operations research at Princeton University. In his popular class, Engineering in the Modern World, Billington considers engineering from scientific, social, and symbolic perspectives. His research interests include the design and rehabilitation of bridges. He is the author of several books, including *Thin Shell Concrete Structures* and *Robert Maillart and the Art of Reinforced Concrete*.

Rutgers University is editing the Papers of Thomas A. Edison. More than six million pages document the experiments and discoveries behind Edison's 1,093 patents.

The Einstein Papers project at the California Institute of Technology (www.einstein.caltech.edu) has published nine volumes of the scientist's papers.

The Darwin Correspondence Project shows how a worldwide network of naturalists helped refine his theory of natural selection. The project has collected 15,000 letters by and to Darwin.

The Guided Studies of Great Text in Science series provides annotated translations of key works such as Ptolemy's *Optics,* Galileo's *Dialogue on the Two Chief World Systems,* and Newton's *Principia.*

The film *Divided Highways* explores how the 42,000 miles of road that became the interstate highway system changed America's physical and cultural landscape.

"Made in America: The History of the American Industrial System," a long-term exhibition at the Henry Ford Museum, looks at how the country became a manufacturing superpower.

More than 120 schoolteachers participated in a summer seminar that studied the French cathedrals of Notre Dame, St. Denis, and Chartres, examining the relationship between the buildings and medieval society.

Films based on David Macaulay's books *Castle* and *Cathedral* illuminate the planning, construction, and function of medieval architectural icons.

The Richest Man in the World, a two-hour film, relates the rags-to-riches journey of industrialist Andrew Carnegie.

The University of Maryland is documenting American labor history through print and microfilm versions of the Samuel Gompers Papers.

Uncovering forgotten stories

Transforming the traditional disciplines

Literary critic Henry Louis Gates, Jr., explores the growing canon of African American letters.

BRUCE COLE: You're described as a cultural critic, a literary historian, various labels. If you were sitting next to someone on a plane and they asked you, "What do you do?" what would you say?

HENRY LOUIS GATES, JR.: I would say I'm a literary critic. That's the first descriptor that comes to mind. After that I would say I was a teacher. Both would be just as important.

I liken the role of the scholar of African American studies today to a Talmudic scholar, someone whose job it is to preserve the tradition, to resurrect the texts and key events of the past, and to explicate them. I've always thought of myself as both a literary historian and a literary critic; someone who loves archives and someone who is dedicated to resurrecting texts that have dropped out of sight. As it turns out, there are a huge number of those texts. At the beginning of my career I didn't realize quite how many there were.

COLE: What kind of history were you interested in then?

GATES: I was interested in American political history. My first degree was from Yale, in history, and John Morton Blum was my mentor. I was the scholar of the house. There are twelve scholars of the house at Yale, and I was one of the twelve. You are relieved of all courses for your senior year, and you are able to write a book, in my case, or compose a symphony or paint a portrait or create a ballet, whatever it may be.

The only stipulation if you were chosen for this project was that you take the year off, that it was not an academic year, hence a five-year B.A. I went to Tanzania, where I worked at a mission hospital for a year.

COLE: You were supposed to do something not academic?

GATES: Not academic. When I came back, I had to declare a major, and I realized that I had taken six history courses and you only need twelve for a major, so I said, "Wow. I'm halfway there." I decided to be a history major, a subject that I had always loved.

COLE: In your memoir, you write about the closeness of your family in Piedmont.

GATES: When I was a kid growing up, my friends wanted to be Hank Aaron or Willie Mays. I wanted to be a Rhodes Scholar. I didn't know why. I just wanted to go to Harvard or Yale, and I wanted to go to Oxford or to Cambridge.

So armed with my Mellon Fellowship, I went off to the University of Cambridge, by way of *Time* magazine. I had written to the head of correspondence at *Time* magazine and said I was a columnist for the *Yale Daily News.* I enclosed my resume and a few of my columns. They brought me down to New York and, in two weeks, they gave me a job.

COLE: That is extraordinary.

GATES: The day after commencement at Yale, I jumped on the *QE II* and sailed to Southampton. All summer I wrote for *Time* magazine.

Anyway, I went up to the University of Cambridge, and then I fell in love, not with history, but with the study of English literature. There was an African there called Wole Soyinka, who thirteen years later would become the first African to get the Nobel Prize. To me he was just a bushy-haired African who wore dashikis. I didn't know who he was.

It turns out that he had fled Nigeria, having been imprisoned during the Biafran War for twenty-seven months, twenty-four in solitary confinement. He wrote a prison memoir called *The Man Died.* After he got out of prison and the book was published, the government was trying to kill him all over again, so he fled to Cambridge. It wasn't really a pleasant experience because the English department denied him an appointment. They said African literature was, at best, sociology or socioanthropology, but it was not real literature.

As he writes in the preface to a series of lectures he gave that year at Cambridge called Myth, Literature, and the African World, I was his only student. I fell in love with African and African American literature.

COLE: There have been other influences as well.

GATES: I've worked with Raymond Williams and with the great George Steiner, and a man called John Holloway. I realized that if I could combine my love for archival work with the theoretical developments that were sneaking their way across the English Channel from France and the Continent, maybe I could make a contribution to both the study of literature in the academy and to a nascent field that was perilously close to dying called Afro-American studies.

COLE: Obviously, you've had inspiring teachers, who have led you in certain directions and have given you great training and the like. Let me ask you about yourself as a teacher. What do you teach and what do you find the relation is between teaching and your criticism and your scholarship?

GATES: I mentioned John Morton Blum, who more than anyone else is responsible for my even entertaining the idea remotely that I could be a writer, and my debt to him will never adequately be repaid. He's a person I love.

Most of my mentors have been white people, outside of my mother and father, because I grew up in an Irish-Italian town, a paper mill town, and there just weren't any black teachers. I had one black teacher in twelve years, and she was the typing teacher. So it has never ever occurred to me that to be a mentor one must look like one's subject or share the same religion. One must just share a similar sensibility and, fortunately, that's not defined by ethnicity or gender or sexual preference or religion or any of those other things.

COLE: Yale in the 1970s was a world unto itself.

GATES: One of the great things about going to Yale was the library. I remember when I first walked in the Sterling Memorial Library, I thought it was the cathedral.

COLE: It is kind of a church, isn't it?

GATES: Yes. I said, "What's that? Is that the church?" And they go, "The church? Dummy, that's the library." I walked in and saw miles of card catalogs.

Then at the Beinecke Rare Book Library, where eventually I would write my Ph.D. thesis—with a pencil because pens aren't allowed in the Beinecke—I realized that there was a huge archive on African American arts and letters called the James

Weldon Johnson Collection. The great photographer Carl Van Vechten had been responsible for creating it.

There I found all this material on Bessie Smith. I was always fascinated with the blues, and I wrote a paper for William McFeeley on her. He asked to see me and he said, "This is exactly the kind of scholarship, combining archival work with interpretation, that we want to see in this new field." Remember, at this point, Afro-American studies as a discipline was two months old, three months old.

COLE: Right.

GATES: And he said, "That's what we want to see happen." You know, not just political rants, as was the wont at that time and continues to be at some places.

Then later I had two fantastic black professors: Charles Davis, who was the first black master of John C. Calhoun College at Yale and the first black American to get tenure in the English department. The other was the great historian John W. Blassingame, who unfortunately died prematurely.

We became best friends. He was a tremendous inspiration to me. From Wole Soyinka and George Steiner, to John Blum and John Blassingame, you can see that I've been blessed with a rainbow coalition of mentors.

COLE: How does your teaching inform your research and vice versa?

GATES: Blassingame taught me a couple of principles. One was: teach what you write, write what you teach. The second one was: give it as a lecture, do your research, prepare it as a lecture, give it all year, as many times as you can, because then it becomes like second nature to you. You can realize the flaws.

COLE: You keep clarifying it; you have to articulate it.

GATES: One of the reasons I started writing for the *New Yorker* was that I'm addicted to writing, but I couldn't really do the kind of archival research that I wanted to do, particularly in the first four or five years that I was here because it was such hard work building the department. I started writing for the *New Yorker* because I didn't have to go to the library to do that.

COLE: Right.

GATES: I would interview people, and it was a different kind of writing, though it was very challenging, and it was a lot of fun. But I'm particularly pleased with the results of my research on the novel by Hannah Crafts, the finding of this 1850s novel *The Bondwoman's Narrative*. It's like I've come full circle from twenty years ago. Nineteen eighty-two is the year that I found and authenticated Harriet Wilson's book, *Our Nig*. Now this second long-lost novel will be published.

COLE: I want to diverge a bit. You had said you wanted a chance to talk about the NEH and the role it has played in your life.

GATES: I had this crazy idea in 1979 that Anthony Appiah and I—I was age twenty-nine and he was twenty-six—we could be W.E.B. DuBois's legatees and edit the *Encyclopedia Africana*. Joe Duffy [former NEH Chairman Joseph D. Duffy] was there when I decided to do a huge research project called The Black Periodical Literature Project.

I needed to get this thing jump-started, and Duffy gave me a chairman's grant. Every two or three years, I would get another grant. It was through that that we were able to restore thousands, literally thousands, of black authors to the canon of American and African American literature. It was through the good graces of the NEH.

COLE: That's very gratifying to hear. I think the review process at the NEH is the jewel in the crown here.

GATES: It's just the truth. The institutionalization of Afro-American studies has been enabled by the NEH to a greater degree than by any foundation.

If you look at the great papers projects, twenty years ago there were no collected papers of African American scholars or thinkers or public figures or writers. None. Zero. Nada. Today, the Marcus Garvey Papers, the Frederick Douglass Papers, the Martin Luther King, Jr. Papers, the black abolitionist papers, the Freedman's Bureau Papers, all of those were supported by NEH.

COLE: The publication of these papers is one of the most important things we do. We're very, very proud of those papers.

GATES: I am, too. Blassingame's role in the creation of the Frederick Douglass Papers and the coalition that he put together with the heads of each of those other papers projects were very influential in shaping my understanding of the agenda for Afro-American studies as we sought to move it from a feel-good politically based, ethnic cheerleading orientation to a real academic discipline.

COLE: You've got to take credit for some of that yourself.

GATES: Well, I could never do that. But the thing I'm proudest of is that for us African Americans it is not just about making a contribution to African American studies. We are transforming the traditional disciplines as well. The notion of what constitutes the canon of American literature is fundamentally different now because of the growth of Afro-American studies or the growth of women's studies.

Henry Louis Gates, Jr., describes himself as a literary critic first and a teacher second. Director of Harvard's W.E.B. Du Bois Institute, Gates is the author of twelve books, including *The Signifying Monkey* and *Thirteen Ways of Looking at a Black Man*. He earned a bachelor's degree in history from Yale University and master's and doctorate degrees in English literature from Cambridge. Gates was the recipient of a MacArthur Foundation grant and a National Humanities Medal. He was the 2002 Jefferson Lecturer in the Humanities.

Stanford University is editing the Martin Luther King, Jr. Papers, which include the civil rights leader's correspondence and sermons. The website (www.stanford.edu/group/King/) provides audio clips of King's speeches.

The Black Periodical Literature Project has microfilmed more than 150,000 pieces of fiction, poetry, book reviews, and literary notices from 900 periodicals dating from 1827 to 1940.

The Freedmen and Southern Society Project at the University of Maryland is assembling more than 50,000 documents charting the transition of African Americans from slavery to freedom.

The Frederick Douglass Papers Project brings together the abolitionist's speeches, and writings. Douglass's papers are being edited by Indiana University-Purdue University at Indianapolis.

The Trans-Atlantic Slave Trade Database helps historians map the origin and eventual home of slaves brought from Africa to America from 1650 to 1867.

A CD-ROM from the Asia Society of New York enables students to explore the Silk Road, a trade route that once spanned 5,000 miles from Turkey to China.

NEH, the National Science Foundation, and the Smithsonian Institution have launched Documenting Endangered Languages, a multiyear initiative to preserve some of the 3,000 languages that are heading toward extinction.

The Emmy-winning documentary *Heritage: Civilization and the Jews* chronicles the 3,000-year history of the Jewish people from their exodus from Egypt to the creation of Israel.

Dennis Tedlock won a PEN Translation prize for his rendering of *Popol Vuh: The Mayan Book of the Dawn of Life*.

The exhibition "Ways of the River: Arts and Environment of the Niger Delta" shows how the river has shaped the lives of the tribes who have called the delta home for more than 5,000 years.

On the writing of biography

The eternal fascination of who

Meryle Secrest describes
the attraction of unfolding
someone's life in print.

BRUCE COLE: You're a well-known and successful biographer.
How did you get to be that?

MERYLE SECREST: If I had stayed in Britain, I couldn't have.
For women of my generation, it was a very, very class-structured
society. My father was a tool and die maker. My mother was a
factory worker. By British standards they were working class.
Nobody in my family had ever gone to university.

My good luck was to get into a secondary grammar school. I
was there for seven years, and I didn't have Greek, but I had
Latin and French. I had a very good education.

I think my career as a biographer really started when I found
Romaine Brooks. I went to the National Collection of Fine Arts
one day, and I saw this self-portrait by a woman I'd never heard
of, and I was absolutely ravished by the work. It's black and
white and gray, and the woman is standing in the foreground
with a black hat, a rather mannish costume, and just a touch of
red hair. I thought, "Who in the world is this person and why
would she be painting this kind of self-portrait?" It's one of those
who-is-it questions that eternally fascinates me.

I did a piece for the *Washington Post* about her. Then I did
another piece for the Smithsonian about her. The director of the
National Collection of Fine Arts, Adelyn Breeskin, was asked by
Doubleday to do a book. Adelyn said no, and she mentioned
me. The editor and I spoke, and the editor said, "You should
fictionalize this." And I said, "You can't fictionalize this. No one
would believe it. It has to be written as a biography." That's
how I got started.

I wanted to see where Romaine had worked. She'd worked
in High Street when Whistler was there. She'd worked in
Paris when Cocteau was there. She had her debut at the
Gallery Duran, where Mary Cassatt had shown twenty years
before, in 1909.

I went to Paris and saw her haunts. I went to Nice, I went to Florence, and I did it all on five thousand dollars, which you couldn't do nowadays.

I managed to match up each chapter with a drawing: Romaine on the Riviera, Romaine in the château. She was a very wealthy girl, and she had a schizophrenic mother and a crazy brother. She was a rejected child. I felt I could empathize.

COLE: After Romaine Brooks, what happened? How did you pick your other topics?

SECREST: We were out for dinner in London, and Francis King—a very nice man, a fine novelist and critic—said to me, "Who are you going to do next?"

I said, "Well, I don't know." But I had done all this work for the National Gallery, and I said, "I really am terribly interested in Bernard Berenson because I keep hearing about Berenson this and Berenson that."

I loved Botticelli and da Vinci and so on, so I'd always had this thing for Berenson. And Francis King says, "I think that's a great idea."

I managed to sell the idea to Holt Reinhardt. I don't know when I first started thinking about how I would frame it, but I had been talking by then to Kenneth Clark, whom I had, in fact, interviewed and who had become a dear friend.

Anyway, we talked about this Berenson idea, and then he sent me a letter saying, "Aren't we going to have fun with our book?" I thought, right. The nuances there did not escape me. I thought, "If I've got K behind me—everyone called him K—I'm off," and I dedicated the book to him.

He was the one who first said to me, "You've got to look at these attributions because you've got to realize that Berenson was a dealer." What he meant was that many of Berenson's judgments were suspect because he was being paid 25 percent of the profits from the sales of Italian Renaissance works. He was authenticating for dealers like Joe Duveen, who was the most important art dealer in the world from about 1910 to 1939. He was a colossus in the art market. He had a gallery at 56th and Fifth in New York, which he had built. He had a gallery just off Bond Street, in Grafton Street, in London. It was a beautiful private house, and he had a gallery in a courtyard in the Place Vendôme in Paris. And K said, "You've really got to look at these."

I said, "Well, how do I do this?" I didn't have a clue. It took me two years to figure out how to read catalogues raisonnés. But Fern Shapley has this wonderful catalog of Italian paintings at the National Gallery, and so I applied myself, and K told me of certain paintings that were really doubtful. That's how that book really came about.

The title, *Being Bernard Berenson,* I must say I thought was rather clever because he had this problem of not being able to say he was a Jew and making up all kinds of fibs for the collector Isabella Stewart Gardner about how they both had common Stewart ancestors and that kind of thing. I was sure that Berenson was Faust and Duveen was Mephistopheles. Now that I've written about Duveen, I know it's the other way around.

COLE: That's wonderful.

SECREST: You just never know. With Berenson, the ends justified the means. He was determined to leave his villa in Florence, *I Tatti,* to Harvard. That was his goal almost from the beginning. He was then already in his sixties and thinking about his legacy. And Harvard said, "And how big is your endowment?" And Berenson said, "Whoops, what endowment?" Harvard wasn't even going to think about it without an endowment. I do believe that was the rationale behind a lot of rather sharp deals that they were all making.

But what can I say about Duveen? You'd have to really know him, and I never knew him. My sense of him is that he was acting entirely within the framework of the time.

COLE: A lot of the subjects of your biographies are kind of prickly characters.

SECREST: Yes, they are.

COLE: Is that because they stand out in relief and they're interesting to write about?

SECREST: Yes. I think you have to write about prickly people. What interests me is the mystery of it. What is it about this person that is so paradoxical?

I think the fun of it is how complicated it gets and how one can—painting is the best analogy—how one can put together a composition that contains within it contrary impulses, discordant colors, and unexpected features but nevertheless hangs together as a composition.

K used to say that that is what he thought I could do: write a human portrait. "You're not very good with abstract ideas, are you?" he used to say, which I rather took offense at, I think. But I know what he meant. He said, "You notice other things other people miss."

And I love doing that. I really adored writing about Berenson and Clark and Dalí. I felt tremendously sorry for Dalí. And I loved Frank Lloyd Wright, though I must say I do think he was a kind of black hole sort of person. So many people's lives were ruined—people who were in any way close to him. But what can you do? He's a giant. He was a horror. But he was an amazing figure, Balzacian, you know? He's the great American life story, I swear to you. The book on Frank Lloyd Wright took me five years. I think that I turned upside down a lot of conceptions about Wright that we all had and showed him to be a much more complicated personality.

COLE: Let's talk about the general state of biography today. There is a huge audience in biography. But many of the major biographies are not being written by academics. They're being written by people with your background. I think that in some circles there's some skepticism about biography, that it doesn't deal efficiently with social history and that there are doubts about individual accomplishments, especially in figures like Wright, let's say. Here at the Endowment, as part of our initiative We the People, we've put in place a lecture series on heroes of history because we do think that individuals often can make a difference.

SECREST: Absolutely. I'm convinced.

COLE: Often these heroes are quite ordinary people who, under certain circumstances, perform heroic deeds or accomplishments and the like. I think that these lectures will not only illuminate the individuals, but they'll illuminate the world from which they arise. What are your thoughts on that?

SECREST: I've always been tremendously interested in the person in relation to the period. I don't think you can divorce the person from the social history, from the background, and the influences on him or her. I think that biography, generally—and I include my own in this, although I've tried mightily to overcome it—biographers generally do not pay enough attention to this aspect of their characters' lives.

I've been looking at biographies in quite a concentrated way for the last five or six years, because I've been a judge for the *L.A. Times* on their book awards. My feeling is that one of the single biggest omissions of contemporary biography is a tendency to act as though everybody knows what the background of your subject is.

It takes a very fine biographer, someone like Justin Kaplan, to put that book in context—or Robert Caro or Edmund Morris or any of the great biographers whom we know.

I'm not really interested in—how shall I say this?—simply chronicling a life. I can't be. I'm writing for a general audience. I have to tell a story about the life. That's not too difficult because I love to tell stories.

COLE: Which biographers do you admire? That's the whole range, not just contemporary.

SECREST: Lytton Strachey, it goes without saying, and the people I've already mentioned. I admire very much David McCullough. I admire him tremendously, more than I can say. But the one who influenced me the most was a man named A.J.A. Symons. *The Quest for Corvo*, do you know it?

COLE: I know it, yes.

SECREST: Fantastic. That's what got me started—*Quest*. That's a mystery, you see? Who was this man really? It's so elegantly done. He's quite discursive and digressive, but he does it as a study of discovering who this man is.

He keeps peeling away the layers. He begins with the outside, and he keeps peeling away and peeling away to get to the essence of the man at the end of the book. The way it's designed, you are riveted to the story of this most eccentric and gifted self-deluder.

COLE: Good biography is also an art form. It does rise to the level of art, aside from the story of the subject's life, right?

SECREST: Well, I think it can be an art form. There are a great many choices that go in to the way a piece is structured that are sometimes just instinctive.

COLE: Besides Duveen and Berenson, who are the players in your newest book?

SECREST: Well, there's Mr. Mellon, the man who gave us the National Gallery of Art. I don't think people knew just how outrageous Duveen was with Andrew Mellon. Duveen is a nonstop talker. And he was funny, too. He was terribly, terribly funny.

He couldn't stand Mellon because Mellon, you know, felt the same way about talking as he did about money. He wouldn't part with anything if he could help it. Duveen was really up against it with Mellon.

What he did was he had everybody on Mellon's staff on his payroll: the private secretary and the butler, the cook—who knows—in Pittsburgh and Washington and so on. They would send him missives about Mr. Mellon's being seen to look at something, and then Duveen would just say, "Well, dear fellow, why don't you have it in your house? No money need change hands. Just have a look at it. See if you can get to like it."

COLE: Is this apocryphal or is it true that Duveen rented an apartment in the same building as Mellon and filled it with art for Mellon to look at?

SECREST: It's all absolutely true. It's the cleverest thing he ever did. Duveen is probably partly responsible for the National Gallery. And John Russell Pope, the man who designed it, as you know, was Duveen's favorite architect. We know that Duveen was the one who pushed for the sculpture galleries because Mr. Mellon didn't have any sculpture. But Duveen had a lot and was determined that Mr. Mellon should like it.

It's very lighthearted. We won't call it tongue-in-cheek, but every once in a while I get my oar in, you know, because I just think he's so funny.

Born and educated in England, Meryle Secrest emigrated to Canada with her parents. She began her career as a journalist working at several small newspapers, including the *Hamilton (Ontario) News* in Canada and the *Bristol Evening Post* in England. Working as a freelance journalist in Washington, D.C., Secrest was captivated by a self-portrait by Romaine Brooks in the National Museum of American Art. She wrote a biography of Brooks that led to biographies of Bernard Berenson, Leonard Bernstein, Kenneth Clark, Stephen Sondheim, Joseph Duveen, and Frank Lloyd Wright.

Profiles of more than 18,000 people who shaped American history are cataloged in the *American National Biography*.

Morgan: American Financier, a biography by Jean Strouse, finds other dimensions in a man sometimes dismissed as a robber baron.

Stacy Schiff's Pulitzer Prize-winning biography *Vera* depicts the creative collaboration between the novelist Vladimir Nabokov and his wife.

David S. Reynolds's 1996 book, *Walt Whitman's America: A Cultural Biography,* won the Bancroft Prize.

Joan D. Hedrick documents the rise of an abolitionist in the Pulitzer Prize-winning biography *Harriet Beecher Stowe: A Life*.

The ten-hour radio series *Leonard Bernstein: An American Life* narrates the journey of a composer in twentieth-century America.

At Rutgers University, the Papers of Elizabeth Cady Stanton and Susan B. Anthony capture the spirit of the woman suffrage movement.

Mary Pickford, a ninety-minute documentary, explores the life and business acumen of one of America's first movie stars.

The documentary *Frederick Douglass: When the Lion Wrote History* charts the abolitionist's journey from slavery to activism.

On civility in a democracy

"I've enjoyed about as much of this as I can stand."

Devising manners befitting a republic

Judith Martin considers
the vexing problem
of a young nation
behaving properly.

BRUCE COLE: Have people always been interested in trying to improve their manners?

JUDITH MARTIN: No. Mid-twentieth century America had one of the cyclical attempts to overthrow etiquette. "It's artificial, it's snobbish," it's this, that, and the other. We go through that every once in a while. The French did that after the French Revolution. They act naturally, whatever that is—nobody knows what natural human behavior is—and they express themselves very freely. After the insults start flying, people can't stand it, and they say, "Why don't we have some manners around here?" We're in that period now.

COLE: What I wanted to get at were your historic predecessors, people who wrote books—Castiglione with his *Book of the Courtier* and Lord Chesterfield's letters to his son. He was reviled, right? Samuel Johnson said Chesterfield had the manners of a dancing master and the morals of a whore. Have you heard that?

MARTIN: It's better than the other way around, right? Emerson said he'd rather dine with a scoundrel than someone who had no table manners.

Throughout history there has been the question: How should man live? How should we behave? How should we treat one another? The minute you have a community, you have to have some form of etiquette, of hierarchy, of recognition, just to keep people from killing one another.

Etiquette is older than law and even now divides the realm of regulating behavior with the legal system. There are a lot of problems with that these days because people keep trying to turn over matters of etiquette to the legal system, which doesn't handle them very well.

There has been etiquette throughout history. It melds with other things. It melds with religion. The Bible is full of things that are really etiquette rules, and so are other religious tracts. Every society has to have etiquette.

COLE: You draw a distinction between etiquette and manners and morals, right?

MARTIN: Yes. I also draw a distinction between manners and etiquette, manners being the principles that are eternal, and etiquette being the surface behavior that varies and changes. Manners have a moral basis. Manners are to etiquette as morality is to the law. Matters of serious morality have to be handled by the law because etiquette depends on the consent of the people practicing it. It has no punishment other than social disapproval—on up to shunning—which can be powerful, but it's not as powerful as throwing someone in jail.

COLE: You've been advising Americans on how to behave—how to mind their manners—since 1978. Let's talk about the problem of manners or etiquette in America. Is it confusing because there is no clear rule about one's place in society?

MARTIN: There is no aristocracy that we can copy. You are a historian. You know how aristocrats generally behave. It's not necessarily something you want to copy.

COLE: That's right.

MARTIN: We are in a wonderful position, and we are the greatest influence on manners in the world today because the Founding Fathers explicitly looked at the manners they grew up with, the manners of their time, and realized that they had a very firm hierarchal court basis and were not suitable for a republic. So they all went into the etiquette business. Jefferson wrote about etiquette, Benjamin Franklin, of course, and others. First of all, they had to establish what would be an appropriate protocol for a republic.

The questions they were working on still haven't been solved. For example, how do you express respect for the dignity of high office without looking as if you're kowtowing to somebody better than you? Every president and other officials have to deal with the fact that we are all equal, yes, but we're not all equal in rank, and we want to have some dignity and some order. Jefferson thought, "Well, fine, just throw all the rank out." It was chaos.

Oddly enough, one of the influences on them was Venice because Venice was determined not to have dynasties and despots. It was an oligarchy, but it was a republic, and the citizens had very strong rights. We got from the Venetians things such as not allowing

people to have foreign titles. When a Venetian ambassador came home, he was stripped of all his medals and titles.

COLE: How the Founding Fathers dealt with the new democracy is of particular interest to me. We have an initiative called We the People, with which we're trying to counter what I call American amnesia. Americans, especially our kids, don't know enough about their history.

The Founders had to set the course. Jefferson wrote on etiquette. And so did Washington, right?

MARTIN: Washington copied out the Jesuits' rules, but, yes, he was also always making etiquette pronouncements and even etiquette decisions. I always quote him when people ask, "Well, if your guest is late for dinner, should you wait?" Washington never waited. He said his cook would kill him. He made the original rules of presidential protocol. The president doesn't have to return calls. He would have his levees and receive people, but he did not return calls.

He set up that question of dignity versus equality. And I say *versus* because you have to meld them, but often one works against the other. When he gave the State of the Union address, he sat on a throne in the Capitol. He was very often accused of being arrogant, but he was struggling with the paradox. Even now, every president is accused of either being arrogant or being too folksy.

COLE: It's hard to win. And, of course, there's this whole issue of how they were going to address the president.

MARTIN: Washington favored Your High and Mightiness. He thought that had a nice ring to it.

COLE: I kind of like that.

MARTIN: He kind of liked it, too, but Adams was against it. Somebody pointed out that it was all very well for Washington, who was a tall man, but if there were a short president—and Adams was short—people would burst out laughing. So they skipped that one.

COLE: What about regional differences in manners?

MARTIN: There are a lot less than there were because people move around all the time, and they have the same influences, just as accents are still discernable, but they are less than they were.

You can often trace manners to the conditions of the territory. Frontier manners obviously are a tremendous influence. If you live on a crowded island like England, you want to create artificial space to keep everybody from being all over you all the time. If you're out in the frontier, you need all the help you can get. Instant friendship and openness and cooperation—very nice American attributes—had a frontier basis. Then you have the southerners, who mistakenly thought they were living the English country-house life on their plantations.

COLE: One of the things you write about is the evolution of southern hospitality, which I found fascinating.

MARTIN: The plantation owners thought they were being English country gentlemen, but who was teaching etiquette to their children? The house slaves. The y'all-come-see-me kind of hospitality is an African tradition that they brought over.

COLE: The frontier and issues of space—that's uniquely American, right?

MARTIN: Very much so. Other countries didn't tend to have that kind of space.

Americans made this very deliberate choice that not only is labor dignified, but leisure is undignified. Even if you had inherited an enormous amount of money as a young man and you did nothing, in early America you were—and are—rather disdained.

COLE: Where do writers fit in?

MARTIN: Writers were often an exception, possibly because you don't really work with the hands in the same sense. In many courts, including the English, the Japanese, the Chinese, you had to be able to write poetry and so on. Writing is a highfalutin vocation.

COLE: That's what is interesting about the artists. Artists in Italy could never achieve any kind of elevated status because they worked with their hands.

MARTIN: But the Venetians were an exception to this snobbery. Not only were they very proud of their artists, but the Venetian glassblowers were so highly regarded that their daughters were entitled to marry into nobility.

COLE: I didn't know that.

MARTIN: Glass was economically important to them. Even the top people, those in the oligarchy, were merchants. They were all in trade.

COLE: People, like Bill Gates, who have made vast fortunes still work.

MARTIN: Because it's shameful not to in America. If you just live off your income, people look down on you.

We're all equal. Even the term we use for servants in this country is *help*. It's a polite fiction, you know, that they are just helping us.

COLE: Yes.

MARTIN: There is this wonderful passage in Tocqueville, where he says that the basis of American manners is that between American master and servant, they both know that the situation could be reversed tomorrow.

COLE: What kind of good and bad influences have American manners had abroad?

MARTIN: It's influenced clothing to a great extent. People are much more informal in their clothing. American blue jeans, everybody walking around Europe with these fake American sweatshirts.

COLE: When you're talking about blue jeans and sweatshirts that there is a kind of reversal: that fashion, instead of coming from on high, it comes from—

MARTIN:—it comes from the street now, yes.

COLE: Is that a particularly new thing? Maybe I'm thinking about Franklin and rusticity.

MARTIN: They were also dealing in symbolism in clothing. A lot of people felt that Washington overdressed and that Jefferson didn't dress up enough.

COLE: What about people who dress casually for the opera and events like that?

MARTIN: It undercuts the sense of occasion. Casual Friday was a disaster on many levels. First of all, anybody with any brains realized that there was still a symbolic system, so therefore you didn't really wear the grungy old clothes you wore on the weekend. You had to have a whole other wardrobe, so you could pretend to be casual but still look important.

With it comes an attitude of "I'm my own person." You see it all the time. You go into a store, and the employees will be having a personal conversation on the phone or listening to music, and they feel they don't have to help you.

COLE: Well, clothes make the man, right?

MARTIN: There's also, manners maketh man.

COLE: Are manners more necessary in a democracy than they were in the old aristocracies?

MARTIN: It's a little bit like language: you can't not have manners of some sort. You could have good manners, bad manners, and so on. It's a bit easier in a hierarchal society, where you know automatically how to place everybody and what the proper behavior should be. I-kowtow-to-you-and-you-don't-need-to-kowtow-to-me type of thing. It's harder when you're all equals, and you have no way of knowing the person's place in the hierarchy. However, it's fair, and we all think it's wonderful.

COLE: It's harder, though.

MARTIN: Yes, it's harder. Another thing is that you establish who you are much more through your manners. To use an old expression, somebody who is as drunk as a lord is still a lord, right? But if you're reeling around drunk in a democracy, in a republic, people say that's who you are—you're a drunk.

COLE: I was just thinking . . . My father's highest accolade about somebody was that he was a gentleman.

MARTIN: Exactly. But in court societies you'd be a gentleman by birth no matter how you behaved. That's the point about America—you have to behave like a gentleman to be a gentleman. And surely that is a superior system.

Judith Martin created the Miss Manners column in 1978, answering etiquette questions and illuminating the history of manners and customs. Martin's books include *Common Courtesy: In Which Miss Manners Solves the Problem That Baffled Jefferson* and *Star-Spangled Manners*. She received a bachelor's degree from Wellesley College and spent twenty-five years at the *Washington Post*.

C. Dallett Hemphill's *Bowing to Necessities: A History of Manners in America, 1620-1860* looks at how rituals helped Americans cope with the transition from monarchy to republic.

The Oxford History of the British Empire examines British interaction with other cultures.

The New Netherland Project (www.nnp.org) published more than 5,000 pages of documents from the seventeenth-century colony of New Netherland.

Thoughtful Giving, a project begun by the Maine Humanities Council and joined by the Georgia and Utah councils, looks at the relationship between civil society and the American tradition of philanthropy (civicreflection.org).

The summer seminar "History of Moral Philosophy: Theories of the Virtues in Fourth-Century Athens and Eighteenth-Century Scotland" tackled two pivotal moments in the history of moral philosophy.

The exhibition "Magnificenza! The Medici, Michelangelo, and the Art of Late Renaissance Florence" focused on the family's use of art as a symbol of power.

The Medici Archive is cataloging two centuries of correspondence between the powerful Medici family and its allies and ambassadors, providing insight into the politics and culture of the High Renaissance.

Scholar Lawrence Klein prepared an edition of Lord Shaftesbury's *Characteristics of Men, Manners, Opinions, Times*. Published in 1711, *Characteristics* provides important insight into the thought and culture of the Enlightenment.

In her book *Domesticity in Colonial India: What Women Learned When Men Gave Them Advice*, Judith E. Walsh finds evidence of the influence of British colonial culture on Hindu women in late nineteenth-century Bengal.

"Dante's *Commedia*," a summer seminar for schoolteachers, analyzed Dante's *Divine Comedy* in the context of the history and culture of northern Italy.

On learning from the Greeks

A legacy of politics and poetry

Historian Donald Kagan
discusses our need to examine
the experience of human beings
in times and contexts different
from our own.

BRUCE COLE: What led you to become a historian?

DONALD KAGAN: From the time I was a little boy I found myself reading history when I had a choice. I read a lot of things, but history had a special appeal for me.

COLE: I have this idea—it comes from John Lukacs—that history is our fourth dimension and that we have to be historians. We can't get to work in the morning unless we have memory, a home.

KAGAN: In my judgment, the best history is one that tells a story and combines it with analysis. The natural way for a historian to analyze things includes answering with a tale. The combination of telling an interesting story and answering questions along the way that an intelligent person would be interested in hearing about that's history at its peak, in my opinion.

COLE: If you were cast away on a desert island and you had only one book by a historian—

KAGAN: One book, eh? Oh, that's hard.

COLE: How about two? I'll let you have two.

KAGAN: I guess it's not an accident I spend most of my life reading Thucydides. Most people who are interested in history start with him.

Herodotus is first, but there's a continuity between Thucydides and the way he carried out his work and serious historians who came afterward. He maintains that power. I could not give him up. I love the way he writes.

Beyond that, I would want to have the historical essays of Thomas Babington Macaulay.

COLE: That's very interesting. How about Gibbon?

KAGAN: Gibbon is a more cultivated taste. His style is too fancy for my particular taste. The story is a grand story, but I don't find that as you move along it's as captivating as many others.

COLE: The greatest user of irony ever, though—

KAGAN:—is Gibbon.

COLE: Yes.

KAGAN: No wonder. I don't have proof of this but I'm convinced his favorite writer must have been Tacitus, who has that same quality. But the styles are very different. Tacitus is very terse and ends up with a sting in the tale. I guess Gibbon does a lot of that, too, but Gibbon is wonderfully satirical.

COLE: What led you to your interest in the Greeks in particular?

KAGAN: When I explain it to people, I use the term the *tragic spirit*. The Greeks, unlike most people, were very well aware of two things at the same time. One is that human beings are capable of truly great things—by *great* they meant great good things and great terrible things. They accepted that. At the same time, human beings were not divine. They were mortal, and they were capable, as I say, of terrible things as well as good.

The Greeks really had no sense of immortality. At the same time, they maintained a sense of the importance of human beings and the great beauty of life. In other words, they faced the fact that death would come, and it was terrible, but the fact that death would come did not mean that what we did while we were alive was unimportant. That attracted me enormously.

COLE: What can modern students learn about battles of more than two thousand years ago?

KAGAN: There are some common human things to be learned: one has to do with the uncertainty in human events in general and in war particularly. Surprising things happen, and battles are sometimes the events that reveal that.

The Greeks ought never to have defeated the Persians. We shouldn't have known a thing about the Greeks. Before their civilization emerged, it should have been obliterated by the extraordinary superiority of the Persian Empire. But, at places like Marathon and Salamis and Plataea, they defeated an outfit that outnumbered them in men and resources to the most

astonishing degree. Well, there's something to be learned from that, too.

COLE: The ancient Greeks and democracy are always very much talked about. In what ways are the ancient Greeks foreign or familiar to us?

KAGAN: That's a good historian's question. I can see that you are a true historian because you really always ought to ask that question about anybody at a different place or a different time, "What's the same and what's different?"

We, to some degree, are like what we are because we inherited certain things from the Greeks and the Romans. One of them that's so striking is the whole area of politics.

Politics, as we understand it, was invented by the Greeks. It's a Greek word meaning things that have to do with the polis—a civic community that is made up of individuals, none of whom is the subject of a single master. The people have to, at some point, participate in the decisions of what the community does. We take it for granted that's the normal way.

But that's the abnormal way.

COLE: That's one of the reasons I think that our democracy here is sometimes not valued enough. Democracy seems just to be the natural way of things. But this certainly is not the case.

KAGAN: Even if you look at the Western tradition, it's only been true for a very small part of Western history. You have two hundred, three hundred years with the Greeks. Then you have a couple hundred years in the Roman Republic. And the next time you see it is in the eighteenth century when the United States gets democracy.

COLE: Why do you think this happened?

KAGAN: Ah, that's the miracle of all miracles. I used to say this when I would be joking with the students. I'd say, "This is a miracle." It was the best I could do in the old days, but I've seen an explanation that really appeals to me by a contemporary Greek historian, Victor Davis Hanson. Victor has written a wonderful book called *The Other Greeks,* in which he essentially explains this phenomenon. He connects it with the development of the independently owned family farm, a brand-new thing in the world at the time. It happens roughly at the same time that the Greeks are developing a new style of warfare based on what they call the hoplite phalanx, which is a close-ordered formation of heavily armed infantrymen that to be successful requires the same kind of person as this independent family farmer, who has never existed in the world before.

This same man then soon demands that he participate in the decisions of his community. These three things—citizen, soldier, farmer, an independent family farmer at that—come into being over a century or so. That is what makes possible the whole concept of self-government.

COLE: That's familiar to us. What's foreign to us?

KAGAN: I think immediately of two great gaps between us and anybody in the ancient world. First, the Judeo-Christian tradition was unknown to them. Their approach to ethics, to religion is very different from what the Western tradition has come to be. The other big difference was the Industrial Revolution. I'm wrapping into this the agricultural revolution—these related events that happened in the eighteenth and nineteenth centuries. Why are these so terribly important? Those developments made it possible for human beings to think, as we regularly do think now, about increasing the total amount of wealth available.

The Greeks, like everybody else before them, imagined there was only a certain amount of wealth in this world, and anybody who got more did so at the expense of somebody else.

COLE: A finite amount, a zero sum game.

KAGAN: That's the way they thought about things. Our hopes for peace—which God knows haven't been met very frequently—have to do at least with the notion that it's conceivable that people will not need to fight each other over material things because there may be enough material things for everybody. Such a notion would have been totally foreign to the Greeks. That's one difference.

The other is the Judeo-Christian tradition versus theirs. Here is a simple way of illustrating the difference. If you stopped a Greek on the street in the fifth century or fourth century and asked, "What is justice?" as, indeed, Plato does in his *Republic,* the Greek would give the answer that Plato reports, which is, "Justice is doing good to your friends and harm to your enemies." Both halves of that are equally important. The Sermon on the

Mount hadn't been given, much less heard, and, if the Greeks had heard it, they would have thought it the silliest thing imaginable.

COLE: That's fascinating. Say an undergraduate were to put the question, "Should we still care about the Greeks?"

KAGAN: It's easy enough to make the case, I think, of why intelligent people should want to know about the Greeks. Think of all the things that they invented that we now take for granted. In addition to things like self-government, they invented the writing of history as we understand it. They invented tragedy. They invented comedy. They invented most forms of poetry as we understand them today. They invented the novel. They pioneered in a whole range of sciences in such a way that their way of thinking about the natural environment is the root of science today. No other civilization came up with that.

We want to know how these things came about and what sort of people did this. Fortunately, we have some of the best exemplars in these different fields. If you want to read tragedy, I think Sophocles is not a bad place to go. If you want to read history, Herodotus and Thucydides are very good places to go.

COLE: I know you take the view that history should be preeminent.

KAGAN: Without history we are the prisoners of the accident of where and when we were born.

COLE: We have no bearings.

KAGAN: That's right. I think, by the way, a liberal education is about freedom and that word *liberal* is connected to the word *freedom.* Is this education suitable for a free person? Well, you have to liberate yourself first from the prejudices of the world in which you live. And the word *prejudice* ought not to be regarded as necessarily negative. We couldn't live without certain kinds of prejudices. On the other hand, if all we have is our prejudices, we lack freedom entirely. We need to examine the experience of human beings in contexts and times different from our own.

That can be done by looking at many civilizations. But I think some of them have special advantages: one of them is remoteness. If it's pretty much like ours, it's a little less valuable than one that's not much like ours or has many differences.

COLE: Yes.

KAGAN: On the other hand, if it's too remote, it may seem strange or amusing because we simply can't relate to it. Many civilizations in history are very worthy but so different from ours that we really can't get very far. The Greeks are very useful to us because of the combination of similarity and difference. But many of the things that derived in large part from the Greeks are not a powerful part of the tradition in which we now live, not because people have rejected them, but because people never even heard of them.

COLE: They just don't know about them.

KAGAN: They just don't know anything about it. For me, the most valuable thing in confronting questions facing the world in which I live is to be aware that the Greeks confronted many of these problems. If I had my way, I'd know as much as I could about as many civilizations as possible, because that's the most liberating thing I could do.

Donald Kagan is the Sterling Professor of Classics and History at Yale University, where his course The Origins of War has been a favorite of students for the last twenty-five years. His published works include *The Peloponnesian War, The Great Dialogue: A History of Greek Political Thought from Homer to Polybius,* and *The Fall of the Athenian Empire.* Kagan is a National Humanities Medalist and was the 2005 Jefferson Lecturer in the Humanities.

The Perseus Project (www.perseus.tufts.edu) began as an online database of classical texts, images, and artifacts. An evolving digital library, it now includes resources on the English Renaissance and the history of science.

With the click of a mouse, scholars can access the 12,000 ancient and Medieval Greek texts that make up the Thesaurus Linguae Graecae (www.tlg.uci.edu).

The Vergil Project, an interactive online hypertext database (vergil.classics.upenn.edu), contains materials related to the poet and his works.

The Barrington Atlas of the Greek and Roman World reconstructs the geography of the ancient world using satellite-generated images, historical scholarship, and archaeological discoveries.

"Greek Values in Crisis: Thucydides, Sophocles, Plato," a summer seminar attended by 120 teachers, explored how the Peloponnesian War changed the fabric of Greek society.

Scholars at the University of Chicago are preparing three dictionaries. The *Assyrian Dictionary* provides a lexicon for Akkadian, the earliest known Semitic language. The *Chicago Demotic Dictionary* catalogs the cursive script used by Egyptians from 650 B.C.E. until the middle of the fifth century C.E. The *Hittite Dictionary* covers the earliest written Indo-European language, which was used in Asia Minor from 1650 to 1180 B.C.E.

The Pennsylvania Sumerian Dictionary (psd.museum.upenn.edu) is an online lexicon of the first documented written language, which dates from 3300 B.C.E.

A Comprehensive Aramaic Lexicon covers texts written from 925 B.C.E. to 1400 C.E. in Aramaic, the language of Babylonian merchants and portions of the Old Testament. The lexicon is being prepared by scholars at Hebrew Union College.

From a segregated classroom to the head of America's schools

Rod Paige lists some
ingredients for success
in learning.

BRUCE COLE: Being a teacher and an educator is often described as a calling. What happened in your life that made you want to be an educator?

ROD PAIGE: To put that in context, you've got to have a view of the environment in which I grew up. This was a small, rural, highly segregated community in Mississippi, central Mississippi, farmers all around. My mother was a teacher, and during my elementary days, my father was a principal. The people in the community who were looked up to were teachers. There was the teacher, the preacher, and that was about it.

The community people called my father Professor. It was a lovable term, and they looked up to him. They would come to him with their community problems. At night, after we had supper, it would not be unusual for ten or fifteen of the community kids to be sitting around the table doing homework. It was an education center.

In those hard days of segregation in Mississippi, we were taught that the solution to most of our problems was education.

COLE: I can see that. Education was the American way to improve yourself, to get out of a situation that you don't want to be in, and to expand your horizons for many, many groups who have come to this country.

PAIGE: I can remember when I was the superintendent of schools in Houston, and the first generation of immigrants arrived from Vietnam and Cambodia—they also saw education as a way to get ahead. I see this budding now in a lot of our Asian and European neighbors. They have discovered education as a powerful economic and social tool.

So maybe our parents and people during that time were right. This contemporary environment has lost a little of that punch.

COLE: That has been a characteristic, I think, of our democracy—that for many people it didn't matter where you came from or what your family background was. I'm not saying that it was a level playing field, but through education you could improve your life. You could make your way in the world. So you don't think that that sort of ethic is as strong now?

PAIGE: Definitely not. That whole value system has suffered some erosion. I'm not exactly sure why that is, but I'm facing it a lot in our challenge to close the achievement gap. For me, teaching and learning involves activity on the part of the learner. This level of motivation and student engagement is less strong now than during the period that I talked about but is as strong for first-generation immigrants in the United States.

COLE: You were talking about growing up in this small town. This, of course, was before *Brown*, before the schools were desegregated. Can you tell me what that was like for you?

PAIGE: With the fiftieth anniversary of *Brown versus Board of Education,* I've been asked that question a lot. It brought back a lot of feelings that I thought were gone.

COLE: What kind of feelings?

PAIGE: In my early years, probably sometime toward the end of my middle school days, I can remember the exact thing that caused me to start noticing the difference. It is rather comical, but the first thing that caused me to start getting angry was the fact that they had a nice gym and we didn't have a gym. We could not play basketball on days when it was raining and muddy. We were out on a clay court. Now of all the ramifications about segregation and separate but equal, I get mad about the fact that they had a gym. That was my first real awareness that there was something different going on here.

Then the situation moved to a point of "We're going to show those kids that we are just as good as they are." Every time there was any kind of interaction, our attitude was one of proving ourselves. That carried on through college and maybe even into graduate school.

COLE: I saw a picture of you and your sister at Jackson State. I think it was on the day that the *Brown* verdict was announced. It must be interesting reflecting on that moment.

PAIGE: Yes. That was towards the end of school. We got the word and, of course, on a college campus there were pockets of academic discussions all around. We were going to wake up tomorrow and this world was going to be wholly different because the Supreme Court decision in *Brown versus Board of Education* had come down.

Looking back at it now, you can see how naive those discussions were. We say that you can change laws, but you do not change people's hearts. That takes more time.

COLE: *Brown* was a start. Are we making progress on equal opportunity in education?

PAIGE: I'm troubled about that. I think that saying "denied the opportunity for equal education" may not be appropriate. Going back and reading the history of African American and Negro education, colonial Negro education, antebellum Negro education, Negro education during Reconstruction and forward, there were times when that was really true. I'm not sure that's the case now.

We need to talk now about taking advantage of the opportunities that are here. I lived through an experience where they were denied, and this time certainly does not equate to that period.

Students, maybe, are not investing the kind of energy and engagement into it that we've seen in those more rugged years. As a general rule, we see a thirty-point achievement gap nationally between black and white fourth graders in reading and in math.

COLE: This circles back to what we were talking about before—about the value of education and how you have to understand that if the opportunity is there, you've got to seize it.

PAIGE: Absolutely. That's the perplexing part about our educational circumstances today. I think if it were understood how important this is and how easily it can make a difference in life, then people would be willing to put more effort towards attaining it.

COLE: I think we were both lucky in that we had parents who valued education. I was the first person in my family to go to college. My parents understood that that was the way that you could get ahead, that you needed to get that education. That was drilled into us from the very beginning.

PAIGE: Absolutely. Somebody asked me one time, a long time ago, "Why did you decide to go to college?" I responded, "Because I enjoy breathing." My parents would have killed me otherwise. There was no not going to college. (Laughter.)

COLE: That's right. It was not an option.

PAIGE: It was not an option. So my parents were much like your parents.

COLE: You do visit a lot of schools?

PAIGE: A lot and I always enjoy it.

COLE: Where have you been lately?

PAIGE: One of the most fascinating schools that I visited was in Virginia, in Newport News. I visited a charter school there. It reminds you, once again, of how eager these young kids are to learn. They sit with bright eyes. They're eager to please you. It's just wonderful to be in good schools like that. But something happens as they go into their middle school years and into high school. Something goes away. I don't know what it is.

COLE: You had a lot of on-the-job training before you became secretary. You were a teacher, a dean, superintendent of schools—what makes a good school?

PAIGE: A good teacher and a willing student. This process has essentially three simple parts: the quality of the instructional process, the quantity of the instructional process, the engagement of the student. When I say *teacher,* I include the principal, the counselor, and other people involved because they are all teachers. They all have to have an interest in student achievement

COLE: I don't believe there has ever been another secretary with the kind of background you bring to the job—as teacher, dean of a school of education, superintendent. Obviously, that makes you look at education and your position in a very special way.

PAIGE: Schools are organizations, and they operate according to the same organizational behavior principles that social psychologists and researchers have put out over the years. Now every organization is different. The military has a unique culture. Corporations have a unique culture. And there is a unique culture in a school that is unlike other organizations. When I read through the history of education policy in the United States,

there's an absence of the practitioner's point of view. I believe that's the source of many of the problems that we have had and the reason we have spent a lot of money trying to accomplish things that were not accomplished. There seems to be a mentality that we can see into these schools and know what is going on there. We do not know. Even legislators say, "Well, I visit schools." That is not enough.

A guiding principle—for me, at least—is that we can make policy, we can provide resources, we can encourage, we can cajole, but when and if schools change, they will do so as a result of the people who walk up and down the halls of the schools and look into the eyeballs of the kids. They will not change as a result of what goes on, on the outside.

It is almost like coaching football. You must create an environment where the players are willing to take the pain that anyone takes on the football field in order to get something done. That is part of what has been missing in education policy in the United States.

COLE: What are the essential elements of No Child Left Behind?

PAIGE: I viewed the No Child Left Behind Act the way it was enacted by Congress as a statement by the Congress that here was some impatience here and some dissatisfaction with the result that they had achieved with this huge amount of expenditure over the years. So the No Child Left Behind Act put teeth in the accountability issues that were embedded in law in 1994.

COLE: Let's talk a little bit about history—I remember you telling me you didn't especially appreciate history when you were in school.

PAIGE: When I was being taught history in school, it had to do with memorizing a lot of dates that seemed to have no relevance to me. It was rote, and it didn't come alive. After I graduated from college, I bumped into a little book about the *Amistad* mutiny, and I read it and it was exciting. I ended up reading several books about it because the *Amistad* mutiny had multiple directions: maritime law, ownership of property, the Constitution of the United States, the relationship with Britain, the relationship with Spain. Was this vessel Cuba's or was it ours, or could the officer who captured the *Amistad* own it because of salvage laws? There was a lot going on. Then, I peeked into John Quincy Adams. When you read that kind of material, it makes you want to go back and get other answers. That's where I got my real spark for history.

COLE: That spark. That's a great gift a teacher can give to a student—to somehow get them excited about the subject. You want to get the person you're talking to as excited about it as you are. That's one of the things we're interested in: to get teachers to get that spark. We have a new series we call Landmark Workshops. We're bringing teachers to places where history was made—to Spanish St. Augustine and to Birmingham, all over the country—to bring these K through 12 teachers together with experts at places where history was made to get them that spark. And history is a great story.

PAIGE: That is the key: people love stories. History is a collection of really great stories. When it is approached that way, it is fascinating.

COLE: We've talked about this before, but knowing our history and knowing where we've come from and how the past influences the present is essential for the survival of our democracy.

But it's something that also should be enjoyable. Besides the larger and vital civic component, it also happens to be a lot of fun.

Born and raised in segregated Monticello, Mississippi, Rod Paige was the secretary of the Department of Education from 2001 to 2005; he was the first school superintendent to serve in that office. He earned a bachelor's degree from Jackson State University and master's and doctoral degrees from Indiana University. Before serving at the national level, he was the dean of the College of Education at Texas Southern University and the superintendent of Houston schools. Currently, Paige is a public policy scholar at the Woodrow Wilson Center.

Landmarks of American History, a program of NEH's We the People initiative, offers workshops for schoolteachers and community college faculty on significant historical events at the places they occurred. Subjects examined include:

"Shaping the Constitution: A View from Mount Vernon" gave 250 schoolteachers the opportunity to study George Washington's role in the creation of the U.S. Constitution in his own environs.

"Crafting Freedom: Thomas Day and Elizabeth Keckley, Black Artisans and Entrepreneurs," enabled 350 school teachers to study the lives and handiwork of Thomas Day, a master furniture maker, and Elizabeth Keckley, who was Mary Todd Lincoln's seamstress.

"The Hermitage, Andrew Jackson, and America, 1801-1861" allowed 100 schoolteachers to examine the culture of the young republic through documents at Jackson's home.

"Between Columbus and Jamestown: Spanish St. Augustine" gave 400 schoolteachers the opportunity to explore colonial history at St. Augustine, the oldest European settlement in North America.

Summer Seminars and Institutes explore key texts and topics in the humanities. More than 60,000 teachers have participated. Subjects examined include:

"Mozart: The Man, His Music, and His Vienna" considered Mozart's music, along with the literature, and culture of the city.

"The Maya World" and "The Andean World" explored sites illuminating the civilizations that predate European settlement in the Americas.

"The Great Plains from Texas to Saskatchewan" delved into the major texts that describe the nature of life on the Great Plains.

"St. Francis of Assisi" studied the representations of St. Francis in texts and art as found in the libraries and monuments of Rome, Siena, and Assisi.

"Social History of Colonial British America, 1607-1763" tracked life in America leading up to the American Revolution.

EDSITEment (edsitement.neh.gov) provides teachers with access to the best humanities websites. It also includes 350 lesson plans.

At the ringside of history

"I think heroes are people who take unusual chances"

Physician and painter
Ferdie Pacheco talks about the
Louis-Schmeling fight and Ali.

BRUCE COLE: Who is the smartest fighter you've ever dealt with?

FERDIE PACHECO: Ali, by about eighteen trillion, jillion miles. Ali was so smart that it was almost a disadvantage for him to fight with anybody. He just outfought everybody. He outfought us— I mean he outfought his corner, and he was always right. Here is what makes Ali great. He shows you his mistakes. Then when you come in to take advantage of them, he kills you.

He leans back, and the right hand comes in and you're left wondering what happened to the left hand because you just got smashed with the right hand. You have this package, six foot four, fast as a welterweight, and heavy punching. Nobody had ever seen anybody like that.

I don't know of one heavyweight, including Joe Louis, who could beat him. Joe Louis was very slow, and good fighters gave him a tough time.

COLE: You have said that everybody remembers where they were the night Joe Louis fought Max Schmeling. Where were you that night?

PACHECO: It was the important event of my growing up. This nation was at the height of segregation. A black man couldn't initiate a conversation with a white woman. We had lynchings. But in this fight, for the first time the black people represented America. They represented Americans against the Nazis, who were coming here with their idea of racial superiority. Joe Louis had the effect of putting a drop of chemical into the water and all the color goes out.

The fight that night happened so fast: bop, bop, bop, bop, over. This poor man, he broke his ribs. And Joe was so enigmatic. He just went out and did what he had to do. That's it. Then he put his clothes on and left. He didn't hang around like Ali and all

these people mouthing and jawing about "I am the greatest."
He just put on his robe and left.

COLE: You have talked about how you wanted to paint heroes.
How do you decide that a person is a hero and worth painting?

PACHECO: The current thing is to say there are no heroes;
there are survivors. I think heroes are people who take
unusual chances.

Heroics are doing something unusual that your common sense
would tell you, "Don't do that," and you do it anyway, for
whatever reason, whether to save somebody from a burning
building or whether to take a stand on civil rights when you
know it's going to cost you the election. That's heroics.

There are all kinds. I think Thomas Jefferson was heroic.
George Patton was heroic because, in spite of everybody who
was against him, he fought the kind of war that you needed to
fight to beat the Germans.

People who have a strong feeling of right and are willing to die
for it, or lose their business or lose their job or do it because
they're right, that's heroic to me.

The film *The Fight* shows how
Joe Louis, the son of an Alabama
sharecropper, became an
American hero when he knocked
out the German boxer Max
Schmeling on the eve of
World War II.

The exhibition "Asian Games:
The Art of Contest" displayed
objects and artwork that reflect
the influence of games in society.

The Sport of Life and Death:
The Mesoamerican Ballgame
(www.ballgame.org) is an
interactive website that
allows visitors to explore the
rituals of a 3,500-year-old
team sport.

For seventeen years, Ferdie Pacheco
was the boxer Muhammad Ali's personal
physician. The son of Spanish immigrants,
Pacheco grew up in Tampa, Florida,
where he began drawing at age five.
Pacheco sold his caricatures and cartoons
to finance his education, receiving a
bachelor's degree in pharmacy from
the University of Florida and a medical
degree from the University of Miami.
He has published ten books, including
The 12 Greatest Rounds of Boxing and
Ybor City Chronicles.

The Henry Ford Museum exhibition "Heroes of the Sky" celebrated the inventiveness and daring of early flight pioneers.

"Elizabeth I: Ruler and Legend," examining the life and times of the famous English monarch, is visiting forty libraries.

Two million Americans viewed "The Many Realms of King Arthur." The traveling exhibition also served as a focal point for reading and discussion groups at sixty libraries.

Partners of the Heart, a documentary, follows the paths of two men, one black, one white, who revolutionized heart surgery.

The film *Margaret Sanger* explores the saga of the birth control pioneer; a four-volume edition of her papers is being prepared at New York University.

The life of a poet

The ties between verse and visual art

Anthony Hecht explains the
mysteries and rewards
of a poet's life.

BRUCE COLE: You have said that being a poet is about a mode of life. *Poet* bears with it so many romantic associations. What is your mode of life as a poet?

ANTHONY HECHT: Well, I'll tell you something. A very good young poet named Charles Simic sent me a photograph of Ezra Pound in the 1890s as a very young man. He already clearly had a sense of his vocation as a poet because he's wearing a loose, floppy open shirt with a tie loosely knotted, and he looks terribly bohemian. It's a real style. Yeats, as you probably know, was also rather a dandy—poetical—in his dress. I was much more influenced by W.H. Auden, who believed a poet should be as ordinary as possible and be easily mistaken for a businessman, if possible.

COLE: I'm always interested in how you work, your daily routine. How does one craft poems?

HECHT: I wish I could tell you—I'm not sure I can. It used to be said of Balzac that he kept old apples in the drawer of his desk, and he had only to open the drawer and smell them, and it would instantly allow him to start writing at a terrific pace. I have no such device. There's nothing that instantly sets off some mechanism in me that allows me to write.

Normally, what I would do is to allow several ideas to coalesce and form themselves into some central idea and image that's going to result in a poem. Very rarely is it a single idea. Once at the University of Michigan, I began talking about this poem before I actually wrote it. It's a poem that celebrates the birth of our son, who was born on the fifth of April in Rochester in a blizzard. That weather and the fact that it was unlikely in April coalesced in my mind with all sorts of accidents in the cosmic order, including the death of people in the Vietnam War, which was going on, and the chance of stray bullets killing people. All of that somehow was brought together and assimilated into a single poem called "The Odds." It is about the birth of our son, but about the birth of our son in a time when people were dying in a random, helpless way. It was a composite of themes that would not normally have belonged together but came out in, I think, a pretty successful poem.

COLE: War is a recurring theme in much of your poetry. It's difficult for you, I know, to talk about your own experience in the war, but it underlies your poetry.

HECHT: My part in World War II was a very modest one. I'm very tentative about writing about it because I don't want to try to give the impression that I was a hero or played a major part.

At the same time, it seems to me that some poets have exaggerated the importance of the role that they played. It's important on a serious subject like that not to posture.

I wrote a letter about this to *Poetry* magazine. Let me quote myself, if I may. "The story goes that James Dickey grotesquely exaggerated the extent of his combat experience. But that, in the end, has little bearing on the quality of his war poems. This is not a pleasant truth. Some experiences are so devastating or traumatizing that we feel they ought to be spoken of only by those who have experienced them firsthand, who have earned the right to speak by the forfeiture of enormous suffering."

I have more trouble with someone like Sylvia Plath, as I also said in the letter to *Poetry* magazine. I quoted Seamus Heaney, who said that her poem "Daddy" rampages so permissively in the history of other people's sorrows that it simply overdraws its rights to our sympathy. I agree with this.

So one has to be very tentative and careful and discriminating in writing about the war. You can't go through military combat in the front lines of the infantry and walk away from it as though it never happened. It's a terrifying experience.

COLE: How old were you when you went into the army?

HECHT: I was a sophomore in college. I guess I was nineteen.

COLE: This was a very early formative experience.

HECHT: Let me just say, apropos of that, that it's not an alien subject of poetry. It's what the *Iliad* is about. It's what most of Greek tragedy is about.

COLE: It's what life is about.

HECHT: Yes. So I see nothing that's contradictory about those topics. I don't want to dwell upon them indefinitely, and writing a Greek tragedy is altogether different from writing a lyric poem. In fact, it's possible to have some sort of reconciliation in a great work, in a tragedy, or in the *Iliad*, when Achilles receives the father of Hector, and there is a very, very touching, humane, delicate scene of reconciliation between these enemies. You can't find room for that in a lyric poem. But in the *Iliad* it's very, very beautiful.

COLE: My experience in the visual arts is that often the greatest examples are those that deal with these themes: suffering and pain but forgiveness and reconciliation, as well. I often think that there's an idea that great art somehow has to be not those things but about beauty and lyricism and the like. That is not at all true.

HECHT: Well, Keats says with regard to *King Lear* that Shakespeare is able to reconcile and present everything that is disagreeable because he puts it in a context of beauty and truth.

To a certain extent, *Lear* is one of the most harrowing of all the works of literature. There's a lot of debate about the significance of the last scene. I am convinced that Lear dies deceived into thinking that Cordelia is going to come back to life, which she is not, and that this is the last self-deception that he goes through.

It's a very, very grim play. Nevertheless, it's a play that is full of extraordinary, touching scenes of real love and real devotion of Cordelia for him and him for Cordelia that don't redeem the action on the stage but do something to elevate the spectator or the reader in a way that I find very moving.

That's what good literature can do. It doesn't evade any of the terrible things in life. It faces them and faces them squarely but puts them in a context in which they have a richer meaning than they would as simply raw, descriptive facts.

COLE: That reminds me of Picasso's definition of art: art is a lie that tells the truth. I think that is a wonderful definition. It is the manipulation of all these things that somehow comes up with something that is more than life, yet is the truth.

HECHT: You are an art historian, and I am a poet. Almost from the first, there has been a kind of reciprocal relationship between painting and poetry, which is to say, from medieval times, when the stories of the New Testament were represented in paintings. This was, as it were, a joint working of visual art and a text that was known and recognized.

COLE: Bellini is one of the most poetic of all painters—one of the most subtle and nuanced and in some ways delicate painters. I should preface by saying I think art historians do a wonderful job of talking but so do poets. Often I find the most incisive criticism of painting from poets.

HECHT: I don't know whether that is true or not, but, as you probably know, John Ashbery began by writing art criticism when he was living in Paris. He liked wild and fairly orgiastic artists.

COLE: I'm a fan of many poets' discussion of visual art, and I'm just thinking of why that is so. First of all, to talk about paintings well, you have to find something that's not easy to find—that is, the verbal equivalent of something that is essentially not verbal. There's also the play of imagination, which is an essential part.

HECHT: Ruskin is interesting on the subject, because he does claim, at times, that the task of seeing and seeing accurately is almost the most important act that a human being can perform in life. This is a task, certainly, for good poets as well as for painters; to see with precision, with accuracy, without lying, without exaggeration. This is a very difficult task.

COLE: You spent a lot of time not just in your study writing poetry, but in the classroom teaching it. How do the two come together for you?

HECHT: Well, I retired from teaching in 1993, when I turned seventy. I have to say my feelings about that are complex. There's an enormous relief at not having to correct lots and lots of papers and exams. I do miss my good students.

COLE: Is poetry alive and well?

HECHT: I think it's in wonderful shape. I can offer into evidence the names of a good number of extraordinarily gifted young poets: Brad Leithauser, who was a student of mine at Harvard, and his wife, Mary Jo Salter, both of them excellent poets,

among the best now writing in America. There are others: B.H. Fairchild, Timothy Murphy, Greg Williamson, Joseph Harrison, and Norman Williams. Norman Williams was a student of mine at Yale. He's a very, very fine poet. All seven of them mean that poetry is thriving in this country and doing extremely well.

COLE: What about the venues for publication of poetry? Are there enough?

HECHT: I think anybody who is good enough is bound to get published. Anybody who comes to you and says, "I'm a marvelous poet, but I can't get published" is being deceived about his or her own quality. I have never found a poet of any quality who can't find a publisher, first of all, in journals easily, but then, after that, in book form.

COLE: Do you think there are an increasing number of readers of poetry, as well? Has poetry flourished?

HECHT: It's hard to say what poetry is. In recent years, it's become a performing art. The people who do rap poetry and go to poetry slams are getting up there on the stage and being personalities. Whatever a poet is, the definition is changing rapidly.

COLE: How do you define a poet? What is your definition of a poet?

HECHT: I don't have one, except that a poem, once it's written, should be memorable and enduring. By enduring, I don't mean a hundred years from now. I mean that when you go back and read it a second, third, fifth, and twentieth time, it still has all the power and authority that it had at the beginning.

COLE: That's an interesting observation. I think that's true for any work of art. When you come back it is not only still arresting, but it seems to have changed. It really hasn't changed, but it's a vehicle that allows you to bring your own increasing experience to it, which makes it even more interesting, more riveting. That's one of my definitions for a truly great work of art.

HECHT: I absolutely agree with that. It's a very mysterious quality in great art that it should grow with you, over a period of many, many years. New interpretations can find themselves that completely repudiate earlier ones and that are nevertheless still valid. Shakespeare's plays are a wonderful example of how we see new things in them constantly.

COLE: And each generation sees something different.

It continually is evolving. It's a kind of wonderful, intricate armature, which is then completed by whoever is looking at it. It changes according to age, generation, and the like. What is the contribution that poetry makes to our lives and to our civilization?

HECHT: Ezra Pound had no doubt at all that poetry was, in fact, the insignia of civilization. There have been a lot of people who have felt that, Dr. Johnson among them.

It's been held that we can estimate the value of any particular civilization by the quality of the literature it provides. That's been said more often of literature than the other arts—music or painting—partly because there's a cognitive content in literature. It is a way of articulating the aspirations, ambitions, the hopes, the anguish of people, and it's therefore a valuable record of the state of the soul of a people.

I think one doesn't sit down to write a poem with the intention of registering a people's soul, except if you're Vergil, perhaps, and feel that you have an obligation to the whole of Roman civilization. Ordinary lyric poets just write their poems one at a time and hope that something serious is going to eventuate.

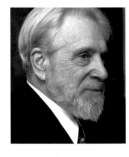

Anthony Hecht had two Fugitive poets as mentors: John Crowe Ransom, who supervised his studies at Kenyon College, and Allen Tate. His published works include *Melodies Unheard: Essays on the Mysteries of Poetry, The Venetian Vespers,* and *The Hard Hours,* for which he received a Pulitzer Prize. The recipient of the Eugenio Montale Award for lifetime achievement in poetry, Hecht was also a gifted translator. His teaching career spanned forty-three years. Hecht died at his home in Washington, D.C., on October 20, 2004.

The literary talents of James siblings William, Henry, and Alice are illuminated in *The Correspondence of William James, The Works of William James,* and *Alice James: A Biography.*

F. Scott Fitzgerald: Winter Dreams, a film that traces Fitzgerald's life from St. Paul to Paris, weaves selections from his works with interviews of those who knew him.

The film *Ernest Hemingway: After the Storm* explores the novelist's struggles to balance a straightforward writing style and a turbulent life.

The 2002 national program *Bard of the People: The Life and Times of John Steinbeck* celebrated the novelist's centenary with exhibitions, films, and public programs.

The William Blake Archive
(www.blakearchive.org) has
digitized the poet's writings,
as well as the paintings he
created to accompany them.

New variorum editions of
*Hamlet, All's Well That Ends Well,
A Winter's Tale,* and *Coriolanus*
document the textual variants,
stage history, and adaptations
of these Shakespearean plays.

The Electronic *Beowulf* Project
at the University of Kentucky is
using fiber-optic technology to
preserve the only extant
manuscript of *Beowulf*.

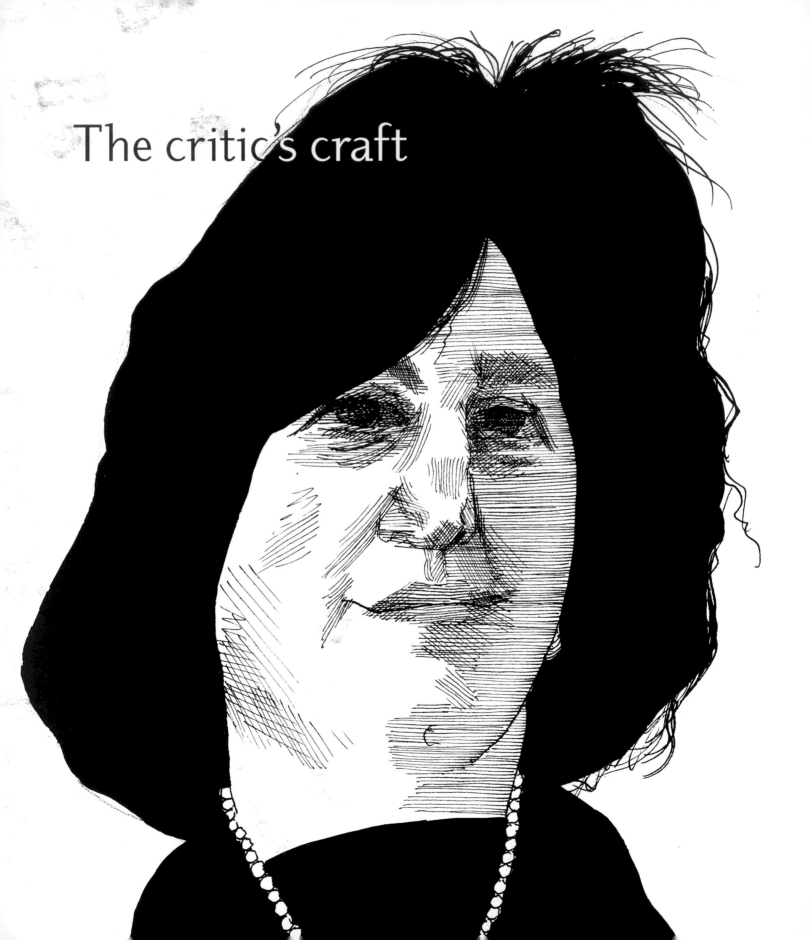

The critic's craft

In the company of poems

Helen Vendler describes
her affinity for poetry and
her path to criticism.

BRUCE COLE: I understand you were pretty young when you embarked on the path that you took to poetry criticism.

HELEN VENDLER: My mother read poetry very intensely to us. She had been a primary school teacher. My father also read poems to us in foreign languages. He was teaching us Spanish, French, and Italian, which is what he taught in high school. He was himself bilingual. He had lived for fourteen years in Puerto Rico and Cuba before he married my mother.

So around me there were languages and lots of poetry, as well as anthologies, all the way from children's ones up through grownup ones, and ones of foreign poetry in translation, too—Mark Van Doren's *Anthology of World Poetry* was where I first ran across Baudelaire in translation, for instance. There was a home library that was basic to me. As was my mother's habit of quoting poetry in conversation. I didn't often know until much later—when I came across a line—that it was Wordsworth's and not hers.

COLE: That's great.

VENDLER: So poetry was around me. I began writing verse when I was six, went on until I was twenty-six, and gave it up in favor of my thesis. I was happier with what I was writing in prose than with what I had written in poetry.

COLE: Do you remember any of the very, very earliest memories?

VENDLER: The earliest were, of course, hymns, because I was brought up a Roman Catholic. We sang the Psalms in antiphonal chorus, in Latin, when I was in high school. These were lyrics that were in my blood, together with the whole Latin liturgy, all the Latin hymns, the *Tantum ergo* and *Adoro te devote* and all that. We sang all that—and the mass. My mother took us to mass every morning, always in a large parish, a requiem mass, and so I heard the *Dies Irae* every morning sung in Latin.

COLE: This is an auspicious launching pad for someone who has spent her whole life dealing with language in many forms.

VENDLER: Yes, because you feel it in the body and not only in the eye, especially when you sing it or do choral recitations. It enters into a kinetic frame.

COLE: People in the past memorized long patches of poetry, right? This is not happening anymore, is it?

VENDLER: There are many things that aren't happening that would make the study of poetry natural to children. First of all, poetry should be taught from the beginning with good poems, not bad poems, and it should be surrounded by a lot of related language arts—memorizing and reciting and choral recitation and choral singing and all those things that feed into the appreciation of poetry.

COLE: I wonder if the skills of memorization have slackened. Since that is not a part of most people's mental furnishings, it's just much harder.

VENDLER: It all depends on cultural values. If you can make schoolchildren in China memorize four thousand characters, you can make schoolchildren memorize anything. Indeed, they memorize on their own all kinds of baseball statistics or popular songs. It's not as though they don't have memories and that the memories can't be activated. It's just a question of will, whether we want to include that as an important part of the curriculum.

COLE: Right. And value.

VENDLER: I've been told that in Japan everybody, before leaving high school, memorizes the hundred great poems in the canon. So of course it can be done. Children's minds are enormously active and retentive.

COLE: Absolutely. Since 1981, you've been at Harvard, where you've been teaching a core course called Poems, Poets, and Poetry.

VENDLER: Yes.

COLE: Tell me a little bit about that.

VENDLER: I try to do nine poems a week, of which the students discuss three in sections, while I try to talk about three in each of my two lecture hours.

Each week, I assign, in addition to old examples, poems of modern poets within the same genre, so students know there are still living people writing elegies or sonnets or nature poetry.

COLE: What dimension does poetry provide that prose can't? Why, at the end of the day, read poetry?

VENDLER: I just had a letter about a talk on this subject given by Seamus Heaney, in which he mentioned the value of learning poems by heart. Otherwise, you need access to a book in which you can track down a poem you once loved, if you haven't memorized it. When you're in a state of perplexity, sadness, gloom, elation, you look for a poem to match what you are feeling.

COLE: What does criticism give to the reader that the poem itself can't provide? As an art historian this is something that is central to what I am interested in.

VENDLER: Well, just as poems are companions through life (once you have read them, heard them, seen them, and internalized them), so it seems to me paintings are companions through life. Who could forget, once you have seen it, the *Death of Adam* of Piero della Francesca? Who could forget Signorelli's *Resurrection of the Body,* about which Jorie Graham has written a wonderful poem? Once artworks are inside you, they reverberate so intensely.

COLE: I believe that some of the absolute finest criticism of art is written by poets. It is so hard to find a kind of visual and emotional verbal equivalent for what you see because, of course, art is not verbal. I think poets have a rare understanding of and ability to express an insight into works of visual art.

VENDLER: Exactly, as they have insight into emotions. Poets have words for those emotions that we don't possess.

COLE: You studied science as an undergraduate.

VENDLER: Yes.

COLE: How does that, do you think, affect your criticism or does it?

VENDLER: I think it's at the base of everything I do. You have to be exact in all your writing in science: your flow chart has to go from beginning to end with all the steps accounted for, and all the equations have to balance out.

Science is very beautiful in its structural shapes, too. Organic chemistry pleased me almost more than anything else because of the three-dimensionality of the assemblage of the molecules and the complication of the organic structures. It was just like seeing the structures of poetry: a molecular branch could go this way, or that way, there could be all sorts of wonderful, complex arrangements.

COLE: This is reflected in your analysis and criticism, which shows a high order of analytical thinking. What do you see as your role as a critic? What do you do to encourage poetry at large, to get us to read, to reflect on what the poet tells us?

VENDLER: When I was young and read poems, I wanted someone to tell me how they got there. The first book of that sort that I read was *Poetry for You* by Cecil Day Lewis. He illustrated how one of his own poems got made, showing many drafts. I didn't know poems had drafts. I thought they just appeared on the page.

The idea that a poem had a history was, for me, exceptionally interesting. It made me curious about manuscripts and about the evolution of any poem. I'm interested in two things: how works of art come to be and how they get better through the author's life, if they do.

COLE: I'm very interested in that myself, the genesis.

VENDLER: The other thing I really feel deeply about the work of criticism is a patriotic impulse of a sort. We have a wonderful patrimony of the arts, as you know, in America and not enough is being done to disseminate it, so that our population will love what has been supplied to them by their artists and writers.

COLE: When I talk about patriotism, I talk about it as a derivation of *patria,* you know, love of place, love of country.

VENDLER: It's easy for people to love the place because they have their home ground and other parts of the country they have visited—the national parks, for instance. But it's harder to bring citizens to love the patrimony of the arts.

COLE: I agree. But I think both are important. We have an initiative called We the People, which is going to provide funds for the study not just of American history but of American culture as well.

VENDLER: That's good. I hope that eventually there will be a sort of sequel from it into classical and past European culture, on which we are naturally so dependent. Perhaps there should be an endeavor of pairing, so that if you read Emily Dickinson, you read some English hymns—that kind of connection.

COLE: Sure. It's important for us to know who we are and what our patrimony is. You also can't make sense of that unless you understand the world around you and where you are in it.

Your dissertation was on Yeats. How did you come to choose him?

VENDLER: I encountered Yeats, early Yeats, at the tail end of Victorian literature. I thought, "Who is this?"

Once you encounter him he makes an enormous impact. When I found him lurking there for me between Tennyson and Eliot, I couldn't believe that there was someone there that I hadn't known about.

COLE: Then you went on to Wallace Stevens.

VENDLER: Yes, a friend made me sit down in a Harvard library to listen to a recording of Wallace Stevens reading his poems. I had skipped over Stevens in my Oscar Williams anthology of modern poetry because I didn't understand the first words of "Sunday Morning," "Complacencies of the peignoir." I thought, "A peignoir can't have complacencies. What is he talking about?"

Then when I heard Stevens read I was struck like Saul on the road to Damascus. This was my poet above all others. This meaning came clearly through the voice as it had not off the page.

COLE: It's interesting how our attitudes change towards works of art. When you come back to them or you think about them they have changed around and you think, how did they change? But, of course, it isn't they that changed. It's you. What role, speaking about these two poets, do you think biography should play in the interpretation of poetry?

VENDLER: We don't know anything about Shakespeare to speak of, nothing that would help us know why he wrote *Hamlet,* and we get along just fine without that biographical knowledge. On the other hand, I don't see any reason to preclude knowing any facts that are out there.

The trouble with giving the biography to students is they substitute it for the poems. It's perhaps cruel to withhold the biography and make them look at the actual words and thoughts on the page. They find it very frustrating. But, at some point, they have to stop thinking, "He wrote this because he lived in Venice," or something of that sort.

COLE: Agreed. When you're not reading as a critic, what are you reading?

VENDLER: I read a lot of art history, to tell you the truth.

COLE: Do you really?

VENDLER: I like to learn things. Since I never had a course in art, I've never been formally trained. What I like to do is get a big heavy book on an artist and work my way through it. Right now I'm reading about Bellini, to whom I became addicted when I spent a month in Venice.

I listen to a lot of music, too. I'm attracted to vocal music, naturally, since I study the lyric. I listen to lieder and opera most. I've begun to understand instrumental music better, and now I'm beginning to listen to Brahms's chamber music.

Helen Vendler has been described as the grand dame of poetry criticism. She has taught for twenty-four years at Harvard University, where she is the A. Kingsley Porter Professor in the Department of English and American Literature and Language. She was the 2004 Jefferson Lecturer in the Humanities. Vendler is the author of numerous books, including *The Music of What Happens: Essays on Poetry and Criticism, The Art of Shakespeare's Sonnets,* and *Seamus Heaney.* She is currently at work on a book about Yeats's styles and form.

The television series *The Shakespeare Hour* features key moments from five plays, combined with historical background and commentary by scholars.

Shakespeare & Company conducted a three-year project on Shakespeare involving institutes, workshops, and curriculum development for Boston elementary and secondary school teachers.

The University of Maryland hosted a three-year program of seminars and workshops on Shakespeare and American literature for 1,300 Maryland secondary school teachers.

The Folger Shakespeare Library brings schoolteachers together every other summer for its "Teaching Shakespeare" institute.

Fellows at the Folger Shakespeare Library have the opportunity to work with 300,000 books and manuscripts dating from the fifteenth to the eighteenth centuries.

The "Shakespeare in Ashland" summer institute teaches schoolteachers how to use classroom-based performances as a teaching tool.

The University of Pennsylvania has preserved and cataloged the Marian Anderson Papers, which contain scores, recordings, and more than 4,000 images documenting the singer's career.

The New York Public Library is cataloging the Jerome Robbins Collection, which includes scrapbooks, costume designs, and videotapes from the choreographer of *West Side Story* and *Fiddler on the Roof.*

Opera in America, the first comprehensive text on the genre in the United States, won the National Book Critics Circle Award.

Louis Armstrong House and Archives (www.satchmo.net) holds 1,600 recordings, 5,000 photographs, and Armstrong's gold-plated trumpet.

The film *Broadway: The American Musical* uses archival footage and interviews with actors, choreographers, and producers to chronicle the evolution of musical theater.

Ken Burns's ten-part film *Jazz* traces the genre's history from Buddy Bolden and Louis Armstrong to Charlie Parker and Wynton Marsalis.

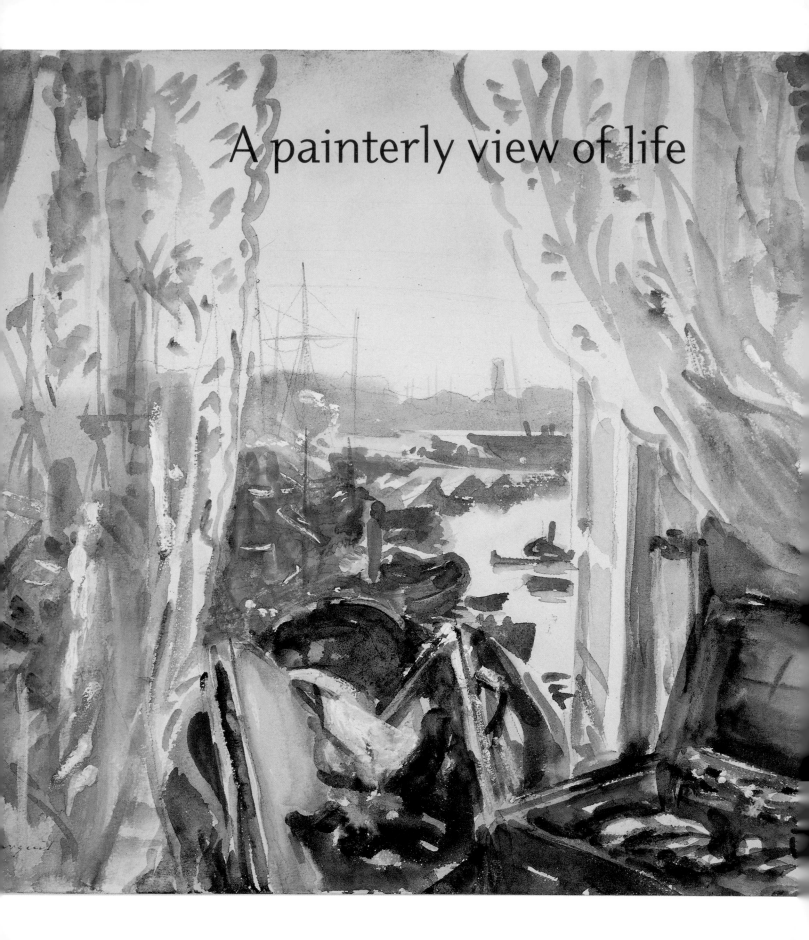

A painterly view of life

How art conveys civilization

Paul Johnson considers
America's sense of adventure
and facility for renewal.

BRUCE COLE: Let's talk about your new book on art. This was something that you'd been thinking about for a very long time.

PAUL JOHNSON: Yes. In it I shift the climax of European art from the early sixteenth century to the early seventeenth century. I think the early seventeenth century was the richest period in the whole history of art, with the largest number of painters and also sculptors. You've got Bernini, who is one of my top ten artists.

COLE: And Caravaggio, of course.

JOHNSON: Yes, Caravaggio, but also Rubens, Rembrandt, Velasquez, Vermeer. There is a tremendous concentration of talent there.

COLE: Do you think that the reason that the early sixteenth century is seen as the pinnacle of art is because it had that great propagandist Giorgio Vasari?

JOHNSON: The whole tradition of art scholarship in Europe is to put that period as the climax. But I don't agree with it because, apart from anything else, it is a period of essentially figurative art. By the early seventeenth century, landscape had arrived, so the range of painting was much wider. They were doing all kinds of new things with light.

COLE: That's very interesting.

JOHNSON: I think art, particularly in the last two or three centuries, has been dominated by western Europe and especially by France. So in the book I show that in the nineteenth century an enormous amount of superb art was produced in the United States and a considerable amount in eastern Europe and in Russia. We've got a new exhibition coming up on Winslow Homer, whom most English people have never heard of.

COLE: A superb artist. Interest in American art has revived recently—for some reason Americans really weren't interested in or were maybe a little ashamed of their art.

JOHNSON: Yes. I think Frederic Edwin Church, with the possible exception of Turner, is the greatest of all landscape artists. He's astounding. There are many others. I've been going through a catalog of the work of Childe Hassam. It is outrageous that he should be tucked away as a minor American follower of French impressionism. His mature style was formed even before he went to Paris.

I would like to see American writers on art stick up for these wonderful painters. Winslow Homer is a very good example.

COLE: Winslow Homer is a sophisticated artist—formal and intellectual—and his work is very exciting.

JOHNSON: Oh, he is. In England, we regard watercolor as particularly our province—and so it is in many ways. But I often say to people that the two greatest practitioners of watercolor in the late nineteenth century were Winslow Homer and John Singer Sargent.

COLE: Sargent has also been coming in for a revival. He's usually seen as a placid, superficial artist. I think we now see him in a very different way.

You were talking about the large issues in your book.

Why should we be interested in art? Why should we devote our lives to it?

JOHNSON: I think art is the oldest thing in human society. Before we could express complicated things in words, we could make art. Art was probably the first profession. Those cave paintings, some of them going back forty thousand years, could not have been done by people who were not supported by the community while they were doing them. That's an important thing—about our self-knowledge as a people, as a race, as a species—to realize that the first real characteristic of civilization was artistic creation.

COLE: I want to ask something along the lines of Sir Nikolaus Pevsner's book *The Englishness of English Art.* What makes American art American?

JOHNSON: I think you Americans started, as you did in literature, with a kind of cultural cringe. Some of the early landscape artists, 1800, 1820, were following patterns that had developed in England and, to some extent, in continental Europe. But you soon branched out on your own. You can't say that a man like Church,

or even Albert Bierstadt, who was, after all, an import—he wasn't born in America—you can't say that they painted in any way except in an American way. That involved grandeur, extravagance, sheer size.

I remember when I first went to America, in the late 1940s. The thing that struck me most about everyday life in America was that everything was bigger. To some extent that is true of American art, too. Things are on a big scale there and they are very daring, adventuresome and there's something fearless about it, which I personally love.

COLE: I agree. There is a kind of spirit and innovation and daring in American art.

I'd like to know a little bit about your background. What led you to the kind of writing you do?

JOHNSON: I was born in 1928. I lived in North Staffordshire in the center of the potteries where, before the war, all the pots that Britain exported all over the world were made.

My father was the headmaster of the local art school, which trained a lot of the craftsmen who made the pots, painted the pots, designed them and so on. He was an artist in watercolor, etching, drypoint, all the traditional processes. I was brought up in the studio.

Then I went to Stonyhurst, which is a Jesuit boarding school in Lancashire. From there I got a scholarship to Oxford, at Magdalen College. I read history there amongst some very good scholars, including A.J.P. Taylor, who taught me modern history.

I got my first job on a French magazine in Paris called *Réalités.*

I met a lot of people in Paris, including Picasso and a lot of writers. In those days France was a great cultural center. After three-and-a-half years I moved to London, worked for the *New Statesman,* which was then the leading weekly and was its editor for five or six years. Then, in 1970, having written a few short books, I decided to become a freelance writer and concentrate on writing big books.

Since then I've written a number of very big books as well as other short ones: *History of the Jews, History of Christianity, History of the American People,* a history of the twentieth century called *Modern Times.*

Finally, having always wanted to write about art, I wrote my book on art, a new history that goes from the time of the cave paintings right up to the present and embraces the whole world. It's mainly a history of western art, of course, because that's what I really know.

COLE: I like it because it's also a very personal book. In that sense it reminds me a bit of Kenneth Clark's *Civilisation*. It's difficult to think about art objectively. You can do that to a certain extent, but then it is really very much a personal view.

JOHNSON: That's true. I studied under Kenneth Clark at Oxford. He was an absolutely wonderful lecturer, a very nice, kind, friendly man who loved young people and wanted them to care as he did about art.

COLE: When I published my first book on Giotto I sent it to Clark, and he sent me back a very nice note and he said, "You have rescued Giotto from the hands of the specialists," which I took as the highest compliment. Don't get me wrong. We need fine-grained scholarship, but we also need to write for people outside our specialty.

JOHNSON: Exactly. One of the consequences of overspecializing is technical writing of a very high boring quotient.

COLE: Your book shows a lifetime of very serious looking. What kind of things do you collect?

JOHNSON: Well, I've never had very much money, but in the 1950s, when I first settled in London after living in Paris, I used to buy drawings by people like Edward Coley Burne-Jones and Dante Gabriel Rossetti and so on, which you could then get very cheaply, as well as watercolors.

COLE: How long have you been painting?

JOHNSON: All my life.

COLE: You started with your father?

JOHNSON: Yes. I used to go out with my father when I was four or five. He used to love drawing churches, and we'd draw churches together. That's when he said to me, "You're not bad, Paul. You can draw a bit, but, I beg of you, don't become an artist. Artists have a rough time at any period, but I can see that this is going to be a particularly bad period for art. Frauds like Picasso will rule the roost for the next fifty years at least." Well, that's proved to be true. He said, "Do something different," so I became a writer.

COLE: But you continue to paint. Watercolor is one of the highest and most difficult art forms.

JOHNSON: It's just so difficult. You have to work so fast. At the end of an hour, I've either got a picture or I've got a mess.

I do also oils occasionally, but I like watercolor because always when I was traveling around the world I could take a little paint box with me and a pad, and if I had half an hour, if I was in Bangkok or Nairobi or whatever it was, I could do a little painting.

COLE: Do you do any portraiture?

JOHNSON: I've tried it. Portraiture is one thing for which you really do need instruction under a master. I've been trying it for years, and I suddenly came across a sentence from Mary Cassatt saying, "With portraits you must start with the eyes." Now it had never occurred to me to do that, but once you know that, it becomes obvious that it's true.

COLE: I love Sargent's definition of a portrait, "A portrait is a picture in which there is just a tiny little something not quite right about the mouth."

JOHNSON: Yes. If I were starting again, if I were now eighteen, I think I'd become a portrait painter.

COLE: I have a quote from you in which you say, "Portraiture is the most humane and fascinating of all the arts."

JOHNSON: It is. You're not going to become a good portrait painter unless you're really interested in people and not just their outward appearance, their face and figure and so on, but what's going on inside.

COLE: Let's turn to your book about the history of the American people. Here at the National Endowment for the Humanities we've embarked on a nationwide program called We the People to encourage learning about American history and culture. Tell me how you came to write this book and about your experience with America.

JOHNSON: When I was at Oxford reading history just after the war—we didn't learn any American history at all—A.J.P. Taylor said to me, "Well," he said, "you can do a bit of American history when you've taken your degree, if you can bear to do such a thing," and he was probably more open-minded than most. There were a lot of great historians at Oxford then, but there was not a single lecture in three years on American history.

One of the ways in which I teach and educate myself and learn things is by writing books.

COLE: My mentor used to say, "If you want to know something, write a book on it."

JOHNSON: I learned an enormous amount about American history in the course of writing this book.

COLE: What particular perspective do you think you bring as an Englishman? That's one of the things I love about Churchill. You get an outside view.

JOHNSON: The great thing about America is that it is the freest country in the world. You people often grumble about restraints on your freedom, but there's nowhere like America in size where there is so much freedom. And because there is so much freedom, you are constantly renewing yourselves. People are encouraged to do new things, and the rewards for doing new things successfully are considerable. So America is renewing itself while Europe is dying on its feet.

America is renewing itself. Its population will be 420 million by the midcentury and bigger, probably, than the whole of Europe by that time, and it is discovering new things.

So when people say, oh, "Germany is going to be the great leader of the world" or "Japan is going to be the great leader of the world"— now they are saying China is going to be the great leader of the world —I say, "Just watch. Wait for the Americans because the Americans will renew themselves again and again and again." You cannot beat freedom for producing ideas, and it's ideas in the end that matter.

The exhibition **"The Legacy of Genghis Khan"** revealed the artistic and cultural developments that resulted from Mongol rule in Asia.

"The Glory of Byzantium" exhibited works from the second golden age of the Byzantine Empire and charted the empire's artistic influence beyond its borders.

"Splendors of Imperial China" brought 350 objects from the personal collections of China's emperors to American museums.

"Courtly Art of the Ancient Maya" gathered the art of Maya city-states of the late classic period.

"Wrapped in Pride: Ghanian Kente and African American Identity" followed the transformation of the ceremonial cloth into a cultural symbol in the mid-twentieth century.

A gadfly in the British tradition, historian and journalist Paul Johnson has been the editor of the *New Statesman* and the *Spectator.* He is a frequent contributor to the *New York Times,* the *Wall Street Journal,* the *Spectator,* and the *Daily Telegraph.* His published works include *A History of the American People, Modern Times,* and *Art: A New History.*

"Major Paintings of Winslow Homer," a summer seminar attended by seventy-five schoolteachers, studied the artist's working methods and use of iconography.

David Tatham's *Winslow Homer and the Illustrated Book* explores how the mechanization of pictorial printing in the 1850s influenced the way Homer painted the world.

The exhibition "Vital Forms: American Art and Design in the Atomic Age, 1940-1960" showed how interest in organic shapes created a new design vocabulary.

"The Great American Thing: Modern Art and National Identity, 1915-1935" looks at how artists on both sides of the Atlantic attempted to create a modern aesthetic of America.

The film *Isamu Noguchi: Stones and Paper* examines the career of the Asian-American artist known for his ability to fuse organic sculptures with architecture.

Isabel Stewart Gardner Museum used a challenge grant to support curatorial and conservation programs in the humanities.

Schoolchildren become online curators at the Seattle Art Museum with a website that allows them to put together an exhibition (www.seattleartmuseum. org/myartgallery/).

Traditions of the table

What food expresses about a civilization

Restaurateur Mario Batali
shares his enthusiasm for
Italian cuisine and culture.

BRUCE COLE: One of the things I think is interesting about your writings and your show is that you talk about food as culture, about the expression of regions and times. Can you talk a little bit about food as an expression of who we are and where we've come from?

MARIO BATALI: Once you become an elaborate and well-developed culture, anything from Rome or the Etruscans, for that matter, the food starts to become a representation of what the culture is. When the food can transcend being just fuel, that's when you start to see these different permutations

In the Italian culture for hundreds of years, as long as Parmigiano Reggiano or prosciutto di Parma has been being made, it's been an expression of not only their hunger and of their love for things that taste good but the artisanship of the products themselves.

COLE: Let's talk a little bit about the history of Italian cooking. Or French food. What does food express about these various civilizations? Of course, French food is all Italian based, right?

BATALI: As they say in Italy, Italians were eating with a knife and fork when the French were still eating each other (Laughter). The Medici family had to bring its Tuscan cooks up there so they could make something edible.

COLE: That's right

BATALI: But that's also a joke. French and Italian cooking have been elevated to a really high art form. The proximity to the Mediterranean I think has a lot to do with that, whether it's been a calming influence or just a generally good thing. Certainly the food is far superior in France and Italy to the rest of Europe.

COLE: Obviously Italian cooking has played a big role in the United States. And you have a new television show about it.

BATALI: The passion of the Italian or the Italian-American population is endless for food and lore and everything about it.

A lot of people I'm meeting around the country speak Italian at home—third or fourth generation and they're still speaking Italian.

My father stopped speaking Italian because his father so badly wanted to be an American. A lot of Italian-American immigrants lost their language and a lot of their tradition, but now it's coming back. It used to be that Italian wasn't cool. Italians were the street sweepers, the marble guys, and the yard guys. Now Italian design is cool with Pavarotti and Ferrari. It's no longer *vergogna* to be Italian.

COLE: I was thinking about the role that food played in your family. I imagine there was a lot of time spent around the table. But it represents more than food, right?

BATALI: Right. It's the whole concept of the supremacy of the family unit in the Italian culture.

When Italians think of the great moments of their life, generally they remember them with a gustatory sense—something that smelled like this or the way that the tortellini were always served on Christmas or on special holidays.

Every region has its own specialties, and whether it was Christmas Eve and the seafood dinner and the seven courses, it's a visceral part of your life. Like myself, when I talk about a great dish, I often get goose bumps. I'm like, "Whoa, I'll never forget that one." The Italians are just like that. It's not all about food. It's part of the memory.

After stints in London at Le Cordon Bleu and as an apprentice to chef Marco Pierre White, Mario Batali discovered his passion for Italian cuisine in the northern Italian village of Borgo Capanne. Today he has seven restaurants in New York City. Batali hosts three television cooking shows and is the author of five cookbooks.

The Kona Coffee Living History Farm, a seven-acre working site in Hawaii, shows visitors how land was homesteaded by Japanese immigrants beginning in 1900.

Hidden Kitchens, a thirteen-part radio series, explores how communities have used food to come together.

"Key Ingredients: America by Food," a traveling exhibition sponsored by the Federation of State Humanities Councils, is visiting one hundred fifty rural communities.

America, The Bountiful, a 2005 chautauqua program of the Missouri Humanities Council, featured George Washington Carver and his contribution to agriculture.

Tupperware!, a documentary that considers how the 1950s plastic container became a cultural icon, won a 2004 Peabody Award.

The book *Hungering for America: Italian, Irish, and Jewish Foodways in the Age of Migration* looks at how immigrant groups adapted culinary traditions to their new country.

The exhibition "The Art of Rice" examined the role rice has played as a diet staple and a symbol of spirituality in Pacific Rim culture over the last 5,000 years.

The evolution of the English language, which at one time made no distinction between sheep—the animals you tend—and mutton—the meat you eat—can be followed in the *Middle English Dictionary* (ets.umdl.umich.edu/m/med/).

Listening to America

An alternative in the world of TV

Brian Lamb talks about his
early days and the founding
of C-SPAN.

BRUCE COLE: Does being a midwesterner in Washington give you a different perspective?

BRIAN LAMB: I felt you had to prove yourself. I don't want to overdo that, but the town isn't the friendliest town in the world. You walk into the town, having been a Purdue graduate, and the first thing they think is you're from a school *out there somewhere*.

COLE: But eventually the various experiences you were having would come together. You had run a successful radio show in Indiana—*Dance Date*, right? When was that?

LAMB: *Dance Date* was in 1961. I did it in my junior year of college. I loved Dick Clark and what he did with *American Bandstand* when I was a kid. When you're young you copy everybody else. I built the sets, hosted the show, got the dancers, sold it to advertisers.

COLE: This marked the parameters of what you were going to do in the future?

LAMB: Absolutely. I started from scratch. In the early days of C-SPAN I did everything. Again, just trying things along the way and eventually you had something, and it either worked or didn't work.

COLE: After school came the navy. What was that like?

LAMB: The navy was probably the most important thing I've ever done. It took me into a world that I'd never been in. We were on the brink of war in Vietnam. I was twenty-two years old, and I was forced to grow up pretty quickly.

COLE: It was total immersion.

LAMB: Total. You wake up one day and you're on a navy ship, a huge ship weighing 13,000 tons, as I remember it, and you have 320 people on board and you are what's called an officer of the deck, at age twenty-two.

I was on a ship for two years and in Washington for two years at the Pentagon. I was in the Office of the Assistant Secretary of Defense for Public Affairs. That was Robert McNamara's information arm—some would call it a propaganda arm.

I was in the audiovisual office, which was responsible for staying in touch and answering queries from the networks: ABC, NBC, and CBS.

In July of 1967, one of the deputy assistant secretaries came in and said to me, "Go home and pack your bag and take this tape recorder with you and fly to Detroit and report to the chief of police's office." Every time there was a news conference with the governor of the state, George Romney, I was to record it and then feed it back over a telephone line to the White House situation room. They would transcribe it and get it to the president.

I'll never forget it. There were race riots, and forty-three blacks were killed in Detroit in July of 1967, and two hundred people were injured. I arrived in the city with, I think, the 82nd Airborne.

There were tanks on the street corners. There were fatigues-wearing military people in the Cadillac Hilton, where we were all staying. It was a bit overwhelming. Even though we were in the middle of the Vietnam War and I was in the military, I had never quite seen anything like this.

COLE: That's fascinating. Did you stay in Washington after?

LAMB: When I got out of the navy in December of 1967, I thought I wanted to be involved in politics. I had been a White House social aide for two years with Lyndon Johnson. I was the guy who introduced the guests who came through the receiving lines.

I interviewed with the Richard Nixon folks in New York, who were gearing up to run in 1968. That didn't work out.

It's just as well. I went back to Indiana, took a job with the old television station I'd been with, Channel 18 in Lafayette, and kind of decompressed. I got the bug in August to go back and worked on the Nixon-Agnew campaign in a very low-level position. I was paid four hundred dollars a month. I was on the road for ten weeks, out in Michigan, Wisconsin, and Minnesota.

That is the only campaigning I've ever done or will ever do. I had gotten a bellyful of it at that point.

COLE: Did you learn things that would be useful to you in C-SPAN?

LAMB: I started down a road of asking the question, "What do I believe in?" What I was involved in was not only unimportant, but it was, I think, a bit of a scam on the public. We would go into a community and spend a week there that would culminate in an event called Speak to Nixon-Agnew, in which the public was invited to come in and tell candidates Nixon and Agnew on an audiotape what they thought were the important issues. The C-SPAN call-in show every morning is the real thing. I was in a position to make a difference so that the public could really be heard, and it wasn't phony.

COLE: Those call-in shows seem more civil than some of the ones I've heard on other networks.

LAMB: People who call are coming into an environment that is much more civil on purpose. We also engage both sides. If you review most of the call-in shows—not all of them, but most of the call-in shows you hear on the radio—they're usually one-sided.

COLE: Let's talk about how C-SPAN got started. Everything that you've talked about foreshadows the creation of C-SPAN, but what was the catalyst?

LAMB: I got a firsthand education about how the media interacts with the government, and it led me to think that there could be a better way. I shouldn't say better way. It was an alternative way.

COLE: How did it turn from a dream into a functioning entity?

LAMB: A man by the name of Bob Rosencrans and another man named Amos Hostetter—they were among those who came together to support C-SPAN in the early days, men who owned cable television systems and were looking for programming. Rosencrans gave me my first check for $25,000, which allowed me to go to all the other members of the business and say, "How about your money? How about your effort? How about—"

It led to this public affairs network we have today. It was started by twenty-two men who gave about $425,000. We had four people who worked there, when we started by carrying the House of Representatives.

COLE: What about that name, C-SPAN?

LAMB: The name C-SPAN was my idea, and I wish I could pull it back. I never liked the name. I made a list of a hundred names, and I ended up choosing C-SPAN because it was the alphabet soup that you had in the business, the ABC, NBC, and CBS. I said, "How can I create a name that will educate people how this is changing?" So I chose the name C-SPAN, which stood for Cable Satellite Public Affairs Network.

COLE: You started with the House of Representatives.

LAMB: Then we added the National Press Club, seventy-five speeches a year. Then we added the Close Up Foundation, meetings with high school students and congressional leaders; we'd do four of those a week.

As time went by and the cable industry got more comfortable, we put more staff on, raised our rates, became a full-time twenty-four-hour-a-day channel. The Senate went on in 1986. We added the second channel C-SPAN2. We now have the third channel C-SPAN3, which is in the new digital environment.

COLE: And you put on call-in shows.

LAMB: Three hours every morning. The idea is to hear from sixty Americans or international callers, sixty voices in those three hours, calling in to experts and members of Congress and the Senate and journalists.

COLE: When did *Booknotes* start?

LAMB: *Booknotes* started in 1989. We put together a program devoted to a hardback book—a nonfiction book—and set up a tradition that we'd only have an author on once. We've had seven hundred different people on since 1989.

COLE: And you have a lot of flexibility. You can take your cameras to many events where there's an important speech or an important discussion, a wide variety of things.

One of the things I think is so wonderful about C-SPAN is that it gives Americans a close-up, unfiltered look at what's going on: how their government functions, what people are saying about current events.

One of the things we're doing here is an initiative on American history. As you know, there's an appalling lack of knowledge of American history: what our institutions are, how the country has developed, who we are as Americans.

It seems to me there is a tremendous interest in history in the general population and in government, which is evidenced in part by that success of C-SPAN. This is a very, very important element in this whole struggle to try to get some more comprehension of who we are as Americans.

LAMB: Well, I'm a work in progress. It's not a case of where I'm the knowledgeable one sitting on the top of the mountain saying, "Listen to me." I'm sixty-one, and for the last twenty-five years I've been involved in this enormous educational process.

I want to make it clear that when I started in this whole thing that I did not have, per se, a goal of improving the country. It's easy for me to say today that the goal was to change television, to democratize television, to hear more voices, to hear more sides.

It takes on a life of its own after you've done it for twenty-five years, as I've done it. I think if it educates people, fine; if we get better voters, which we're not, that would be good, too. But that's not a goal of mine, and we're not social engineers. We try to educate people, but we have a very limited amount of money to do that.

COLE: What's next for you for C-SPAN?

LAMB: There is no identifiable next. The ingredient in C-SPAN that everybody should think about is that we are the only network that doesn't have to make a profit. If you don't take that out of the equation, you could never do this.

I'm not even sanguine about the long-term future of C-SPAN. Who knows what will happen ten years from now? Right now there's a total commitment on the part of the cable television industry and the satellite providers, but what happens if the economic model changes down the road?

COLE: So it's a great job?

LAMB: For me it's the best thing humanly possible. I couldn't imagine anything else or what it would be. I had about ten jobs before I came to this job, and every one of them had some value to what I'm doing now. A lot of them were in this town: UPI Audio for a while, and United States Senate press secretary for a couple of years, three-and-a-half years with Tom Whitehead at the Office of Telecommunications Policy, the two years at the Pentagon and at the White House in the Johnson years—four years with a cable television magazine getting to know the business—all that led up to being this generalist.

Actually, I'm at the age where I spend a lot of time stepping back so that the younger folks who are at C-SPAN can make the decisions and make the place run. If I left tomorrow, we wouldn't have a situation where everybody says, "Oh, he's not here any longer, so C-SPAN can't continue."

Brian Lamb's affinity for broadcasting was evident early, as he worked for radio and television stations in his native Lafayette, Indiana, while attending Purdue University. He served in the navy and then worked as a freelance reporter and a Senate press secretary before settling into public television. The founder and CEO of C-SPAN and a National Humanities Medalist, Lamb continues to host C-SPAN's *Washington Journal* and *Q & A*.

Northwestern University's Oyez, Oyez, Oyez (www.oyez.org) profiles the history, decisions, and justices of the Supreme Court.

The Historical Atlas of Political Parties in the United States Congress, 1789-1988 traces American political leanings.

The Political Commercial Archive at the University of Oklahoma contains recordings of more than 50,000 political ads aired between 1936 and the present.

Newsreels from the Hearst-Metrotone Newsreel Collection documenting global political events during the 1920s and 1930s have been preserved.

Michigan State University's National Gallery of the Spoken Word (www.ngsw.org) is digitizing more than 50,000 speeches, interviews, and broadcasts by people from all walks of life.

Choices for the Twenty-First Century, a series of reading and discussion programs led by humanities scholars in thirty-two states, looked at civic discourse and public policy issues.

The radio call-in show *Storylines America* encourages listeners nationwide to examine their connections to their communities and landscapes.

The website Valley of the Shadow (http://valley.vcdh.virginia.edu/) uses newspapers, diaries, and letters to document how two neighboring communities, one pro-North and one pro-South, responded to the Civil War.

The film *Do You Speak American?* explores linguistic diversity and regional variance among English speakers in the United States.

The New Georgia Encyclopedia (www.georgiaencyclopedia.org) catalogs the history and institutions of the Peachtree state. The website was developed by the Georgia Humanities Council. Other state humanities councils are developing online encyclopedias.

Scholars have assembled encyclopedias documenting the diversity and individual qualities of American cities and regions, including:

The Encyclopedia of Indianapolis

The Encyclopedia of Chicago

The Encyclopedia of New England

The Encyclopedia of New York

Encyclopedia of Southern Culture

Encyclopedia of the Great Plains

The New Handbook of Texas

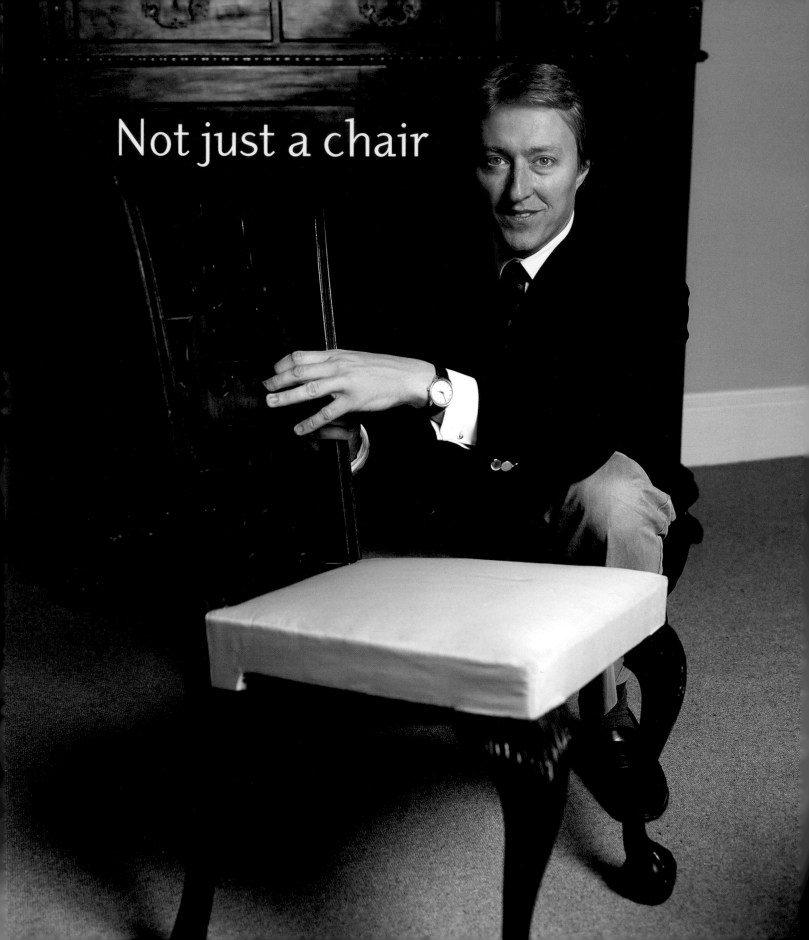

Not just a chair

Deciphering the hidden message of furniture

Leigh Keno explains
the history to be found
in the grain of wood.

BRUCE COLE: People know you from *Antiques Roadshow* and from your book. You've done a lot to raise the knowledge of American furniture in the United States. Maybe you can tell us a little about how you got started.

LEIGH KENO: My brother Les and I grew up in upstate New York, in Mohawk, on a farm. Our parents were antique dealers—Dad still is—and we grew up going to flea markets and riding around the countryside on motorcycles looking for all sorts of treasures. By the age of twelve, we started a diary. It was 1969. It says, "Leigh and Leslie Keno, twelve years old. We are antique dealers."

COLE: One of the reasons that I admire dealers is that they know things on a level that most art historians don't. They handle the object, and they have to make certain kinds of judgments about it.

KENO: Leslie and I at one point in our lives almost went into the museum field. As a dealer, you constantly make decisions on authenticity

You're a well-known paintings expert. You've written some fine books about painting. But even with a picture, I would guess you like to look at the structure behind the canvas.

COLE: Oh, yes. One of the best ways to know something about any work of art is to touch it, turn it around, know it inside and out. It gives you an understanding of the work of art that is much more profound. It's one thing to read about works of art and see photographs, but it's an entirely other thing to confront something in reality. You started by digging objects up and classifying them. This was a way to learn?

KENO: It was. When we brought a piece back, we would take out what books we had and we'd see if we could find it in the book. We had Wallace Nuttings's *Furniture Treasury,* the big blue volume that's about as thick as a New York telephone book. It's what we fell asleep with every night.

We owe a lot to our parents. Our father—Dad's seventy-one—constantly taught us to look at things. If we were driving to get milk at the store, he'd look up at a Greek revival house and say, "Look at that—the cornice on that building" or "Do you see those arches?" I try to do the same thing today with my young son.

The other day, he looked up at the building across the street and said, "Daddy, Gothic. That's Gothic, right?" I told him once that Gothic has a rocket-ship type of window.

So I hope that I can pass on that, what my dad passed on to us.

COLE: You have to understand the things and the physicality of the things. You know that. You've handled literally thousands of objects.

KENO: I learn every day. Every *Roadshow,* for instance, you learn so much just from looking at these objects. If you look at three or four items in a month, signed and dated, made by so-and-so, and from a particular state, you're going to naturally learn about objects from that area or period. It's only by looking at thousands of objects that you get a broad sense of decorative arts.

COLE: I believe that great pieces of furniture are great works of art, comparable to the most important painting or sculpture. I know you feel that way, but can you tell me why that is?

KENO: Can I articulate it? That's the question. Let's take this block-front chest in front of us. It's a Boston block-front chest with a wonderful shaped front and bracket feet. You know this was made by a craftsman. If he had just wanted to make a chest that would hold something, it could have had a straight front, it could be made of pine, and it would have exactly the same function as this chest does. But this chest was made of imported figured mahogany, and these drawer fronts are shaped out of a solid piece of mahogany. The dovetails are beautifully cut. This person was proud of what he did.

The thing about a great piece of furniture is that it just speaks to you. One thing I hope we learn from the *Roadshow* is that a chair is not just a chair and every piece has a story to tell.

COLE: There's also a very sculptural quality to furniture, the way that it moves out into space or the way that space penetrates it. One of the things you talk about that intrigues me is the *personality* of furniture.

KENO: Each piece does have its own personality. The wonderful thing about American furniture is regionalism. We're sitting in a room right now surrounded with various pieces, and to me it's like

sitting at the United Nations with people from several countries, and I can identify them from their clothes or their flag or their accents. This is a Massachusetts clock. This is a New York kneehole desk from 1760. This is a Salem high chest, a Boston veneered dressing table.

COLE: One of the things we're beginning at the National Endowment for the Humanities is an initiative called We the People. We hope to help people in the understanding of our history and of our culture. We want to try to figure out who we are and where we came from and maybe where we're going. Obviously early American furniture is an expression of early American culture. What can you say about that? What makes American furniture American?

KENO: That's a good question. One part of the answer is physical. The woods used are very often American grown. This New England high chest is made of figured maple that almost certainly is American. The secondary wood is white pine, which grew in abundance in New England. Then there are the quirks of the piece: the way the fan is carved, the drop pendants, which are quite eccentric compressed balls with a shaft and a ball below, and the shape of the legs, the shape of the skirt. All of these are distinctly American.

COLE: What does a piece of eighteenth-century furniture tell us about the history of the time?

We can learn many things. For instance, if we look at furniture owned by Quakers in Philadelphia, we find some rather ornate pieces. Despite what we think about Quakers as being against unnecessary displays of wealth, some of the pieces owned by the most prominent families are pretty flashy—high chests with carved rosettes, rococo brasses, and carved fan drawers, pieces made to impress, believe me.

COLE: Would you find regional differences in furniture in England or is that a particularly American thing? Was there a difference in that in London you had one center producing furniture that was then sent out to the provinces, whereas here there isn't that centralization of manufacture or style?

KENO: Right. One thing that I find fascinating in this country is to see which urban area was important at which time of our colonial history. I spent five years doing a study on chairs, on colonial Boston chairs. Two fellow scholars and I had decided that a whole group of chairs that were thought to have been made in Newport and in New York were actually made in Boston. We were going against twenty or more books that said completely the opposite. But we said to ourselves, "Wait a minute, this is an early misattribution that got repeated and repeated and repeated."

The short of it is—that we found that the vast majority of these chairs descended in local families—if the chairs descended in the Van Rensselaer family of New York, the assumption was that they were made in New York. We prowled the shipping records from the 1730s and '40s and early '50s, during Boston's heyday, and found that Boston was to chairs during this period what Detroit was to car making in the sixties—it ruled. These chairs were shipped out by the thousands all down the coast, like ordering today from an L.L. Bean catalog, and not all were inexpensive. The agent in Boston would load the ship up, the chair makers owned partial shares in the ships, and these were shipped, along with clock cases, desks, chests, and other items, down the coast.

COLE: En masse.

KENO: We went to the Public Record Office in London and went through the cargo records of American colonial ships. Most of the copies here were destroyed. It was unbelievable to open these big dusty books with sealskin covers and look at the colonial records that had been sent back to the king. We found great documentation there.

We documented a shipment of chairs right from the Boston dock to prominent New York merchant William Beekman. We found receipts showing that William Beekman was buying chairs in Boston. His upholstered settee, now in the collections of the State Department, had long been attributed to New York because of its provenance. We now know that it is Boston made.

COLE: I think one of the wonderful things about the *Antiques Roadshow* is that you make history come alive. You tell a story by looking at an object, and then figuring out where it was made and who might have made it. It seems to me that's a good way for people, especially young people, to begin to get an understanding of their history. Do you feel that way?

KENO: I agree one hundred percent. A program like the *Roadshow* is wonderful for educating young people about their past, about American history. We do have many younger people coming up to us appraisers on the show. Parents have said, "Thank God for the *Roadshow* because my son would only talk about skateboarding and

hip-hop music and now he's watching the *Roadshow* every Monday night and he's collecting antique toys."

The objects are a catalyst. You have this object. You have people talking about it. It's the most basic way of communicating. It's basically storytelling. And that goes back hundreds and hundreds of years. It goes back to people around the fire telling stories and passing those stories down to their children, who pass it down to their children, who pass it down.

If that can get young people excited—even if it includes prices that get people excited—that's okay. As you said earlier, the nice thing about being a dealer is that it combines the scholarship with the business aspect. If a boy finds that a baseball glove owned by Mickey Mantle that he found for fifty dollars is worth three hundred dollars, that's a nice byproduct. He can go treasure hunting, and at the same time he might learn all about Mickey Mantle and the history of baseball.

COLE: That dynamism, that kind of connection to the object tells history in a way that you can't find in a museum. It is that sense of discovery. I agree with you that the monetary value in a way confirms this—the rarity, the condition and the like.

KENO: That's right. The other thing I want to add is that touching helps the sense of discovery. With my son, I never tell him not to touch something. He picks up almost anything. I probably wouldn't let him pick up a Tiffany lamp, I guess—but he can pick up any chair he wants, if he can lift it, because I think if you tell people, children, not to touch antiques, they'll grow up thinking that they shouldn't touch.

COLE: One of the things I like about the show is that these aren't sacred objects. People handle them, turn them around. You pull out drawers, tip the thing up—and that's actually what they were for. People did handle them. They did look at them, use them.

KENO: Right.

COLE: That's the difference between a painting, let's say, which also tells a story and sometimes has a purpose, like an altarpiece or something similar.

KENO: Yes.

COLE: But it's not something that you use. You don't store stuff in it. It's not functional. That is another dimension of furniture that is very exciting, the utility of it.

KENO: Absolutely it is. A piece of furniture is basically made up of many, many small parts, like a Lego sculpture really. And they're all connected.

COLE: Do you feel when people bring things to the *Roadshow* that you're helping draw their history out of them? They've had this object sitting around their house and they've never really known anything about it. They go to the *Roadshow* and they discover it has all this history.

KENO: You have to find it within. A lot of times, people may know things about their family's history, but they don't know how it connects. They can say, "Well, yes, my grandmother did come from Ireland a hundred years ago, but we always assumed this was made in New York."

And you tell them that, "Well, this is actually an Irish piece."

COLE: A show like the *Antiques Roadshow* or some of the others, I call the public university. They have this wonderful educational value to them. Obviously people are hungry for those kinds of shows on PBS and the History Channel. They're hungry for a kind of public history, for an exciting story.

KENO: I think the idea of traveling across the United States on a treasure hunt and finding—and seeing people from all over the United States—is part of the fun. A lot of times it's not about the price, not about the money either. It is about the history and the stories.

Education and training workshops for preservation professionals teach the latest conservation techniques to preserve and care for humanities collections.

More than 45,000 institutions have received an **NEH** disaster wheel, a spin-the-wheel guide with capsule information on salvaging collections after a natural disaster.

Museums and archives across the country have improved the storage and environmental conditions of more than 33 million objects.

Leigh Keno, on right, began collecting wrought-iron hinges from old barns as a child and never lost his interest in antiques. He and his twin, Leslie, a senior vice president at Sotheby's, have become fixtures on *Antiques Roadshow*. After working at two auction houses, Keno opened his own gallery in New York City, specializing in eighteenth and early nineteenth-century American furniture, decorative arts, and paintings. He received a bachelor's degree in art history from Hamilton College and was a visiting scholar at Winterthur Museum.

To celebrate Thomas Jefferson's 250th birthday, artifacts and works of art that once belonged to Jefferson were exhibited at Monticello. The exhibition drew 635,000 visitors over a seven-month period.

Andrew Jackson's home, The Hermitage, was restored with the help of a challenge grant. Archaeologists have also unearthed portions of nine slave dwellings.

One hundred schoolteachers attended a summer seminar at The Hermitage examining documents connected to Andrew Jackson's presidency.

A challenge grant helped the Winterthur Museum, Garden, and Library preserve its collection of more than 85,000 objects made or used in America between 1640 and 1860.

"A Grand Design: The Art of the Victoria and Albert Museum" showcased 250 pieces of decorative art from around the world.

Canterbury Shaker Village used a challenge grant to restore two original Shaker buildings and construct an education center.

An odyssey of learning

Scaling America's academic world

Vartan Gregorian recounts

his amazing journey from

Iran to the presidency of

the Carnegie Corporation.

BRUCE COLE: You've just written your autobiography. Tell us how that came about. How did you decide to do that?

VARTAN GREGORIAN: It was a hard decision. I was brought up in a culture in which you don't discuss family affairs with strangers. My grandmother had a marvelous saying: The reason houses have four walls is to keep all information inside. At the same time, I wrote the book as a tribute to my grandmother and all the other people who played such a crucial role in my life. Without them, I would not be here.

I also wanted to write about the foot soldiers of civilization— teachers whose impact seldom gets acknowledged. They come without name, and they remain unknown.

I wanted people to know that life is not all cynical, that there are kind, wonderful people who do good things, help other people out of a sense of humanity, charity, religious obligation, ethnic pride, whatever.

COLE: Tell us about some of these strangers and how they pointed you on the road to today.

GREGORIAN: The first stranger who entered my life was Edgar Maloyan, the French vice-counsel in Tabriz. He was a Gaullist. He came to Tabriz in 1948 to open a consulate. He told me, "You have to go to Beirut, Lebanon. You're too smart to stay in Tabriz."

COLE: That's your hometown.

GREGORIAN: Yes, my hometown. I told Mr. Maloyan, "I have no money to go to Beirut." He said, "Don't worry. I'll take care of it." I believed in him. I think later he was amazed that somebody could put such trust in him. He gave me three letters of introduction. Then, with fifty dollars, I went to Lebanon.

A second stranger, an optometrist in Tabriz, gave me his property deed. That allowed me to obtain a passport because my father had told me if I could get a passport on my own, he would let me go, assuming that no fourteen-year-old kid could get a passport.

This optometrist took me under his wing. He was the pro bono agent for many Armenian newspapers published in Iran and abroad. I used to help him by distributing American, French, Egyptian, Greek, and other Armenian newspapers published in Fresno, Boston, Athens, Marseilles, Paris, and Cairo. As I distributed the newspapers, I also read them.

COLE: So you were a newspaper delivery boy.

GREGORIAN: Yes. It helped me also because I got to read. I got to know the world from the perspective of diaspora.

A third stranger was the head of the Armenian Relief Society of Lebanon. She found out that I was practically starving and helped me secure a dining facility for five dollars a month. It offered meals at noontime and dinner but no weekends. Out of nowhere there appeared three families in Beirut—Armenian expatriate families from Iran—who invited me to eat all my meals with them one day a week. So I had three meals with them. Then, finally, as luck had it, I met the director of the Collège Arménien whose eyesight had diminished, so I became his second pair of eyeglasses. That helped me secure room and board at the Collège Arménien.

Another stranger was my English teacher at the school, who filled out my applications to Stanford and Berkeley. Both schools accepted me. Stanford sent its response by airmail; Berkeley sent its by surface mail, so I ended up at Stanford. In Palo Alto, an Armenian family adopted me for Sunday meals and holidays. All of this reinforced my conviction that diasporas are not ghettos— rather they are connecting bridges to larger communities, be it Jewish, be it Irish, be it Chinese, Armenian, Indian, and so forth. I never realized that until then.

COLE: What was it like when you got to Stanford?

GREGORIAN: I thought it would be another American University of Beirut—small student body, some nice buildings, tranquil, looking over the Mediterranean. I was just blown away coming to Stanford. It was almost like a small, self-contained city. The number of students, the number of faculty impressed me, but also the fact that most students had cars. I never imagined that a student could be rich enough to own a car. In my hometown, there were three families who owned cars: they were the head of the telegraph company, the head of the bank, and a millionaire who was the head of a factory. But to have students have cars,

and for me later to be able to buy a car, a used car, oh, my God! I took pictures of myself in front of the car, posing.

More important than the cars or the affluence was the attitude in the classroom: I was astonished to find that students were able to question professors. I never, ever imagined that in the middle of a lecture, I would raise my hand and say, "Excuse me. What do you mean by Chaucer's saying such-and-such?" In the tradition I came from, you took down what you were told and then repeated it. When I was asked, "What do you think?" "Do you understand?" That was an alien experience for me.

COLE: You had a long university career, and you also spent eight years at the New York Public Library. Did you ever dream of anything like that?

GREGORIAN: No. The first time I set foot in the New York Public Library was in 1956, in August. I walked along Fifth Avenue. I went to see St. Patrick's Cathedral, and then I walked down to the New York Public Library and went in. I was too ashamed to ask, "Where is the admissions desk?" I just headed toward a familiar sign: the Slavonic division. I walked in, and nobody asked me for an ID, so I thought I had entered there illegally; quietly and quickly I left, hoping nobody would catch me. . . . I never knew that the library was free, that it was the people's palace, that you had the right to just go in. I never imagined one day I would be president of the New York Public Library.

COLE: What do you think in your career had prepared you to take that job?

GREGORIAN: From childhood on in Tabriz, Iran, I loved books. To be in a place with twenty-five to thirty million items, for a poor boy who had no books, to be put in a position to open the doors and lend books to millions of people—it was an intoxicating dream that I never would have anticipated.

While at Penn, I made the university librarian a professor of English and bibliography so that the librarian was formally one of the faculty.

A librarian must not just know where what book is located or how to retrieve information. They have to be mediators between the book and the scholar; they should be able to say, "I can tell you that the first edition had three lines extra." They need to be scholar-librarians who love books, who also know details, how to communicate, and how to serve.

COLE: Did you do any teaching when you were at the New York Public Library?

GREGORIAN: Yes. I taught European intellectual history at the New School, and I loved it.

COLE: You kept teaching at Brown?

GREGORIAN: Yes. I taught a freshman seminar and a senior seminar, and I taught a course on Alexis de Tocqueville with Professor Stephen Graubard, who is from Brown's history department and the editor of *Daedalus*.

COLE: Was it hard to be intellectually engaged as a university president?

GREGORIAN: Let me put it delicately. The difference between being a university president and being head of a library I can sum up this way: books don't talk back. Everybody's grateful for any additional book you bring, any additional hour you keep the library open. And I went to every party to be the public face of the library everywhere.

COLE: The public face.

GREGORIAN: Yes. I sat on all kinds of committees to prove that the library was a central part of the life of the city, and therefore I was interested in the city's welfare, not just the library's. So I was very busy.

COLE: So, it's been, what, six years since you've been away from Brown? Before we turn to your work at Carnegie Corporation, I wanted to talk about the state of education in general. I think of you as someone who is not only a humanist but also someone who is a strong supporter of educating people in the fullest sense: to educate the mind and the heart and to make people question and have perspective. What's your assessment of where we are? How are the liberal arts faring?

GREGORIAN: Well, I'm worried about what's happening. Consciously or unconsciously, there has emerged a perception in the United States that somehow liberal arts should be for elite institutions and that your community colleges and your big state universities and others should concentrate on careers rather than on learning, per se. The higher the tuition goes up, the more parents tend to say, "What's the earning power of a degree going to be?" That worries me. Our democracy may have an aristocracy of talent, as Jefferson said—which is fine—but we don't want

everyone else to be left out. Something like that seems to be happening, though.

Now, more than ever, the university has to teach you how to learn and to teach you not only what you know but also what you don't know. At one time I thought of giving a diploma that said, "Congratulations for knowing this much, and now we instruct you to learn for the rest of your life," just to make the point that we are sending the graduate into the world with a map, with a compass, to go and learn.

COLE: You open their eyes to what they don't know—I think that's very true—while at the same time giving them a foundation.

GREGORIAN: Yes, a foundation. The other thing that worries me is the lack of perspective and the confusion that reigns about the differences between job and career, what is an amateur and what is a professional, the confusion between leisure and free time. These are classical concepts that are no longer being dwelled upon.

COLE: At Carnegie Corporation of New York, you've had role reversal. Instead of asking for money now, you're giving it away. Tell me about that?

GREGORIAN: The difference is the following: I don't have to please people anymore, even though I still am pleasant. I also don't—how should I put it politely—I don't have to entertain except with friends. At the same time, there are other activities. I'm involved internationally now, whether it's in Afghanistan, whether it's Africa, India, Pakistan, central Europe, or Russia. I'm involved in all of them.

People think that giving away money is an easy job. Actually, it's harder than raising money, as you well know, because you have so many excellent projects that compete for funding. The issue is, as I tell our staff, "Are we going to be an incubator or an oxygen tank?"

Foundations have to be in the idea business, not the need business. Everyone has needs.

And finally, we have to prepare the next generation of leaders, scholars, and thinkers. What are we doing to accomplish that? As a matter of fact, yesterday I put some fundamental questions to my colleagues. I asked, "What are we doing? Why are we doing what we're doing? How well are we doing it? Are we the right people to do it? If another foundation is doing a better job, why can't we give the money to them to do it? Are we capable of illuminating failures we've had that we can publicize in order to protect others from committing the same mistakes?" All of those issues are fundamental to how you evaluate success, especially in scholarship. How do you inculcate the love of learning, the love of excellence, while helping institutions and organizations? Competing priorities are always there: How do you balance the national and international factors, the local and regional, the needs of the City of New York after 9/11? I thought it would be easy to come here and just write checks, but I found it just as difficult as being a fund-raiser.

An additional difficult task with regard to dealing with money is how to take maximum advantage of it—something I'm not intrinsically familiar with because I come from a culture of scarcity. This was driven home to me when I was visiting universities in Africa. I was struck by the fact that some classrooms, for example, did not have proper blackboards. Immediately, I thought, "How many official luncheons in New York City, if they were canceled, would provide how many blackboards in Africa?" Being a product of a culture of scarcity compels you to accept moral responsibility and forces you to prioritize the use of your scarce resources.

In my office, I have Andrew Carnegie's picture looking always at me, and I think he's saying, "All right, boy, what are you doing? How come you're doing what you're doing? Is it going to make a difference in matters of knowledge and world peace?"

COLE: You're finding this worthwhile.

GREGORIAN: I'm having a wonderful time.

Vartan Gregorian emigrated to the United States in 1956 and quickly began ascending the rungs of academia. He taught at the college level before becoming president of the New York Public Library and later, Brown University. The president of the Carnegie Corporation of New York, Gregorian was a National Humanities Medalist and received the Medal of Freedom, America's highest civil honor.

The Library of America, which began with seed money from NEH, publishes the work of America's foremost writers, among them Willa Cather, Henry James, Mark Twain, and James Baldwin. Since 1979, the library has published 156 titles and a total of 6 million copies.

More than 1.1 million books deteriorating because of acidic paper have been microfilmed to preserve their intellectual content.

Book festivals supported by state humanities councils:

Arizona Book Festival

Baltimore Book Festival in Maryland

Great Basin Book Festival in Nevada

Great Illinois Book Fair

Great Salt Lake Book Festival in Utah

The Montana Festival of the Book

North Carolina Literary Festival

Northwest Bookfest in Washington

Rocky Mountain Book Festival in Colorado

South Carolina Book Festival

Southern Festival of Books in Tennessee

Texas Book Festival

Virginia Festival of the Book

The documentary *Out of Ireland* traces the plight of the more than 2 million Irish emigrants who came to America between 1845 and 1855.

The film *Africans in America* follows the lives and struggles of slaves and free blacks from colonial times until the Civil War.

The film *Ancestors in the Americas* tells the story of Asians who immigrated to the United States from the 1700s to the 1900s; some of the first arrivals were Filipino sailors who jumped from Spanish galleons and settled In Louisiana bayous.

Chairmen of the NEH

NEH is headed by a chairman who is appointed to a four-year term by the United States president, acting on the advice of and with the consent of the Senate.

BARNABY C. KEENEY
July 1966 to June 1970

RONALD S. BERMAN
December 1971 to
January 1977

JOSEPH D. DUFFY
October 1977 to
December 1981

WILLIAM J. BENNETT
December 1981 to
February 1985

LYNNE V. CHENEY
May 1986 to January 1993

SHELDON HACKNEY
August 1993 to August 1997

WILLIAM R. FERRIS
November 1997 to
November 2001

BRUCE COLE
December 2001 to present

National Council on the Humanities

The National Council on the Humanities acts in an advisory capacity to the Endowment, reviewing grant applications and making policy recommendations. The members serve six-year terms, and are nominated by the president of the United States and confirmed by the United States Senate.

Herman Belz
Jewel Spears Brooker
Celeste Colgan
Dario Fernández-Morera
Elizabeth Fox-Genovese
Craig Haffner
Nathan O. Hatch
David M. Hertz
James Davison Hunter
Tamar Jacoby
Harvey Klehr
Andrew Ladis
Wright L. Lassiter, Jr.
Thomas Lindsay
Iris Cornelia Love
Wilfred M. McClay
Stephen A. McKnight
Lawrence Okamura
Ricardo J. Quinones
James R. Stoner, Jr.
Marguerite H. Sullivan
Stephan A. Thernstrom
Jeffrey D. Wallin

Jefferson Lecturers

Sponsored by NEH, the Jefferson Lecture is the highest honor the federal government bestows for distinguished intellectual achievement in the humanities.

1972
LIONEL TRILLING
"Mind in the Modern World"

1973
ERIK ERIKSON
"Dimensions of a New Identity"

1974
ROBERT PENN WARREN
"Poetry and Democracy"

1975
PAUL A. FREUND
"Liberty: The Great Disorder of Speech"

1976
JOHN HOPE FRANKLIN
"Racial Equality in America"

1977
SAUL BELLOW
"The Writer and His Country Look Each Other Over"

1978
C. VANN WOODWARD
"The European Vision of America"

1979
EDWARD SHILS
"Render Unto Caesar: Government, Society, and Universities in Their Reciprocal Rights and Duties"

1980
BARBARA TUCHMAN
"Mankind's Better Moments"

1981
GERALD HOLTON
"Where Is Science Taking Us?"

1982
EMILY T. VERMEULE
"Greeks and Barbarians: The Classical Experience in the Larger World"

1983
JAROSLAV PELIKAN
"The Vindication of Tradition"

1984
SIDNEY HOOK
"Education in Defense of a Free Society"

1985
CLEANTH BROOKS
"Literature and Technology"

1986
LESZEK KOLAKOWSKI
"The Idolatry of Politics"

1987
FORREST McDONALD
"The Intellectual World of the Founding Fathers"

1988
ROBERT NISBET
"The Present Age"

1989
WALKER PERCY
"The Fateful Rift: The San Andreas Fault in the Modern Mind"

1990
BERNARD LEWIS
"Western Civilization: A View from the East"

1991
GERTRUDE HIMMELFARB
"Of Heroes, Villains and Valets"

1992
BERNARD M W. KNOX
"The Oldest Dead White European Males"

1993
ROBERT CONQUEST
"History, Humanity, and Truth"

1994
GWENDOLYN BROOKS
"Family Pictures"

1995
VINCENT SCULLY
"The Architecture of Community"

1996
TONI MORRISON
"The Future of Time: Literature and Diminished Expectations"

1997
STEPHEN TOULMIN
"A Dissenter's Story"

1998
BERNARD BAILYN
"To Begin the World Anew: Politics and the Creative Imagination"

1999
CAROLINE WALKER BYNUM
"Shape and Story: Metamorphosis in the Western Tradition"

2000
JAMES M. McPHERSON
"'For a Vast Future Also': Lincoln and the Millennium"

2001
ARTHUR MILLER
"On Politics and the Art of Acting"

2002
HENRY LOUIS GATES, JR.
"Mr. Jefferson and the Trials of Phillis Wheatley"

2003
DAVID McCULLOUGH
"The Course of Human Events"

2004
HELEN VENDLER
"The Ocean, the Bird, and the Scholar"

2005
DONALD KAGAN
"In Defense of History"

Heroes of History

Part of the We the People initiative, the Heroes of History Lectures provide Americans an opportunity to learn about the lives and endeavors of our national heroes. Inaugurated in 2003, the lecture is given annually.

2003
"Ordinary Heroes:
Founders of Our Republic"
ROBERT V. REMINI

2004
"Abraham Lincoln,
American Hero"
HAROLD HOLZER

Charles Frankel Prize

In 1988, the Endowment established the Charles Frankel Prize to honor individuals who have made outstanding contributions to the public understanding of the humanities. The Charles Frankel Prize was awarded annually from 1989 through 1996.

1989
PATRICIA L. BATES
DANIEL J. BOORSTIN
WILLARD L. BOYD
CLAY S. JENKINSON
AMÉRICO PAREDES

1990
MORTIMER J. ADLER
HARRY HAMPTON
BERNARD M.W. KNOX
DAVID VAN TASSEL
ETHYLE R. WOLFE

1991
WINTON BLOUNT
KEN BURNS
LOUISE COWAN
KARL HAAS
JOHN TCHEN

1992
ALLAN BLOOM
SHELBY FOOTE
RICHARD RODRIGUEZ
HAROLD K. SKRAMSTAD, JR
EUDORA WELTY

1993
RICARDO E. ALEGRÍA
JOHN HOPE FRANKLIN
HANNA HOLBORN GRAY
ANDREW HEISKELL
LAUREL T. ULRICH

1994
ERNEST L. BOYER
WILLIAM KITTREDGE
PEGGY WHITMAN PRENSHAW
SHARON PERCY ROCKEFELLER
DOROTHY PORTER WESLEY

1995
WILLIAM R. FERRIS
CHARLES KURALT
DAVID MACAULAY
DAVID McCULLOUGH
BERNICE JOHNSON REAGON

1996
RITA DOVE
DORIS KEARNS GOODWIN
DANIEL KEMMIS
ARTURO MADRID
BILL MOYERS

National Humanities Medal

Inaugurated in 1997, the National Humanities Medal is bestowed by the president of the United States on individuals or groups whose work has deepened the nation's understanding of the humanities.

1997

NINA M. ARCHABAL
DAVID A. BERRY
RICHARD J. FRANKE
WILLIAM FRIDAY
DON HENLEY
MAXINE HONG KINGSTON
LUIS LEAL
MARTIN E. MARTY
PAUL MELLON
STUDS TERKEL

1998

STEPHEN E. AMBROSE
E.L. DOCTOROW
DIANA L. ECK
NACYE BROWN GAJ
HENRY LOUIS GATES, JR.
VARTAN GREGORIAN
RAMÓN EDUARDO RUIZ
ARTHUR M. SCHLESINGER, JR.
GARRY WILLS

1999

PATRICIA M. BATTIN
TAYLOR BRANCH
JACQUELYN DOWD HALL
GARRISON KEILLOR
JIM LEHRER
JOHN RAWLS
STEVEN SPIELBERG
AUGUST WILSON

2000

ROBERT N. BELLAH
WILL D. CAMPBELL
JUDY CRICHTON
DAVID C. DRISKELL
ERNEST J. GAINES
HERMAN T. GUERRERO
QUINCY JONES
BARBARA KINGSOLVER
EDMUND S. MORGAN
TONI MORRISON
EARL SHORRIS
VIRGINIA DRIVING HAWK SNEVE

2001

JOSE CISNEROS
ROBERT COLES
SHARON DARLING
WILLIAM MANCHESTER
RICHARD PECK
EILEEN JACKSON SOUTHERN
TOM WOLFE
NATIONAL TRUST FOR
  HISTORIC PRESERVATION

2002

FRANKIE HEWITT
IOWA WRITERS' WORKSHOP
DONALD KAGAN
BRIAN LAMB
ART LINKLETTER
PATRICIA MacLACHLAN
MOUNT VERNON LADIES' ASSOCIATION
THOMAS SOWELL

2003

ROBERT BALLARD, PH.D
JOAN GANZ COONEY
MIDGE DECTER
JOSEPH EPSTEIN
ELIZABETH FOX-GENOVESE
JEAN FRITZ
HAL HOLBROOK
EDITH KURZWEIL
FRANK M. SNOWDEN, JR.
JOHN UPDIKE

2004

MARVA COLLINS
GERTRUDE HIMMELFARB
HILTON KRAMER
MADELEINE L'ENGLE
HARVEY C. MANSFIELD
JOHN SEARLE
SHELBY STEELE
UNITED STATES CAPITOL
  HISTORICAL SOCIETY

Pulitzer Prizes for work supported by NEH

The Pulitzer Prize was established by Joseph Pulitzer's 1904 will to encourage excellence in journalism. Administered by the Columbia University Graduate School of Journalism, the prize categories honor print and online journalism, arts, and letters.

1975
History
DUMAS MALONE
*Jefferson and His Time,
Volumes I-V*

1976
National Reporting
JAMES RISSER
Des Moines Register

1979
History
DON E. FEHRENBACHER
*The Dred Scott Case: Its Significance in
American Law and Politics*

National Reporting
JAMES RISSER
Des Moines Register

1986
Biography
ELIZABETH FRANK
Louise Bogan: A Portrait

1987
History
BERNARD BAILYN
*Voyagers to the West: A Passage in the
Peopling of America on the Eve of the Revolution*

1989
History
JAMES M. McPHERSON
Battle Cry of Freedom: The Civil War Era

1991
History
LAUREL THATCHER ULRIC
*A Midwife's Tale: The Life of Martha Ballard,
Based on Her Diary, 1785-1812*

1995
Biography
JOAN D. HEDRICK
Harriet Beecher Stowe: A Life

1996
History
ALAN TAYLOR
*William Cooper's Town: Power and Persuasion on
the Frontier of the Early American Republic*

1997
History
JACK RAKOVE
*Original Meanings: Politics and Ideas
in the Making of the Constitution*

1999
History
EDWIN G. BURROWS
AND MIKE WALLACE
Gotham: A History of New York City to 1898

2000
History
DAVID M. KENNEDY
*Freedom from Fear: The American People
in Depression and War, 1929–1945*

Biography
STACY SCHIFF
Vera (Mrs. Vladimir Nabokov)

2002
History
LOUIS MENAND
*The Metaphysical Club: A Story
of Ideas in America*

2004
Biography
WILLIAM TAUBMAN
Khrushchev: The Man and His Era

History
STEVEN HAHN
*A Nation Under Our Feet: Black
Political Struggles in the Rural South
from Slavery to the Great Migration*

Credits

p. i Old Post Office Building, Washington, D.C. where NEH has its offices, © Bob Rowan, Progressive Image/Corbis

p. iv Jaime Wyeth, *Ida Proper* watercolor. Used with permission of the artist

p. 6 David McCullough, © Richard Frasier
p. 10 David McCullough, © Richard Frasier
p. 11 Gilbert Stuart, *George Washington* (Lansdowne portrait). Oil on canvas, 97.5 x 62.5 in. National Portrait Gallery, Smithsonian Institution /Art Resource, NY
p. 12 George Catlin, *River Bluffs, 1320 Miles above St. Louis*. Oil on canvas, 28.5 x 36.6 cm. Smithsonian American Art Museum/Art Resource, NY
p. 16 Gary Moulton, courtesy of the University of Nebraska-Lincoln Photography
p. 17 Charles Christian Nahl and Frederick August Wendroth, *Miners in the Sierras*. Oil on canvas, 137.7 x 169.8 cm. Smithsonian American Art Museum/Art Resource, NY
p. 18 Excavation of a portion of the *Arabia*'s stern, © David Hawley
p. 24 David and Greg Hawley, © Walter Whittaker
p. 25 Mask of Tutankhamun, Scala/Art Resource, NY
p. 26 World Series at Yankee Stadium, 1957, © Bettmann/Corbis
p. 28 Winston Churchill inspecting air raid damage to Battersea, south London, 10 September 1940, © Hulton/Archive by Getty Images
p. 32 Lukacs, courtesy of John Lukacs /photography by Tobias Everke
p. 33 Eisenhower addressing troops, 6 June 1944, AFP/Getty Images

p. 34 Leonard P. Zakim Bunker Hill Bridge, ©Andy Ryan, courtesy of the National Steel Bridge Alliance
p. 38 David Billington, courtesy of the Princeton University Office of Communications
p. 39 Golden Gate Bridge under construction, used with permission of the Golden Gate Bridge, San Francisco, CA, www.goldengatebridge.org
p. 40 Interior of Sterling Memorial Library, Yale University, © Michael Marsland
p. 44 Henry Louis Gates, Jr., © Jared Leeds
p. 45 The Buddha Shakyamuni as an Ascetic, jade ca. 1940-1949, Avery Brundage Collection, © Asian Art Museum of San Francisco
p. 46 Bernard Berenson before Antonio Canova's *Pauline Bonaparte* in the Borghese Gallery in Rome, Magnum Pictures
p. 50 Meryle Secrest, © Marion Ettlinger
p. 51 Suffragettes posting bills, glass negative, 5 x 7 in. Courtesy of the George Grantham Bain Collection, Library of Congress
p. 52 © William Hamilton cartoon, the New Yorker collection, the William Hamilton cartoon bank
p. 56 Judith Martin, © Paul Fetters
p. 57 Giorgio Vasari, Studiolo of Francesco I de Medici in the Palazzo Vecchio, Florence, Scala/Art Resource
p. 58 Douris Painter, red figure kylix ca. 490 B.C.E., Erich Lessing/Art Resource, NY
p. 62 Donald Kagan, © Michael Marsland
p. 63 Bill of sale, Hittite, seventeenth century B.C.E. Baked clay, 12 x 6 cm. Erich Lessing /Art Resource, NY

p. 64 Rod Paige with schoolchildren, courtesy of the U.S. Department of Education
p. 68 Rod Paige, © Jennifer Crandal
p. 69 Interior of Vienna's Waisenhauskirche on Rennweg, where Mozart performed before Empress Maria Theresia in 1768. Erich Lessing/Art Resource
p. 70 George Bellows, *Stag Night at Sharkey's*. Oil on canvas, 92.1 x 122.6 cm. Courtesy of the Cleveland Museum of Art, Hinman B. Hurlbut
p. 72 Ferdie Pacheco, © Steve Satterwhite
p. 73 Otto Lilienthal Gliding, 1896. Henry Guttmann/Getty Images
p. 74 Henri Matisse, *Blue Interior with Two Girls*. Oil on canvas, 25.75 x 21.25 cm. Used with permission of the University of Iowa Museum of Art, gift of Owen and Leone Elliot
p. 78 Anthony Hecht, © Dorothy Alexander
p. 79 William Blake, *Song of Los*, Copy C, Bentley Plate 5. Relief etching with color printing and hand coloring. © The Pierpont Morgan Library/Art Resource, NY
p. 80 © David Levine, caricature of Helen Vendler, originally published in the *New York Review of Books*, November 1996
p. 84 Helen Vendler, © Mark Morelli
p. 85 Marian Anderson singing on the steps of the Lincoln Memorial, Easter Sunday 1939, © Bettmann/Corbis

p. 86 John Singer Sargent, *View from a Window, Genoa*. Watercolor with pencil and oil, 40.3 x 53 cm. HIP/Art Resource, NY
p. 90 Paul Johnson, © Isabel Hutchinson
p. 91 Winslow Homer, *Palm Tree, Nassau*. Watercolor, 54.5 x 38 cm. Metropolitan Museum of Art
p. 92 Paul Cezanne, *Still Life with Basket or the Kitchen Table*. Oil on canvas, 25.65 x 31.50 in. Réunion des Musées Nationaux/Art Resource
p. 94 Batali and Cole, © Mike Ciesielski
p. 95 Ando Hiroshige, *In the Rice Fields*, from the series *Fifty-Three Stages on the Tokaido*. Color woodblock print, 34.0 x 22.8 cm. Réunion des Musées Nationaux/Art Resource, NY
p. 96 Brian Lamb, AP/World Wide Photos
p. 100 Brian Lamb, courtesy of C-SPAN
p. 101 Original photograph of Captain Bollerman's kitchen, Chambersburg, PA, ca. 1864, U.S. Army Military History Institute, from Valley of the Shadow
p. 102 Leigh Keno, © Max Yawney
p. 106 Leslie and Leigh Keno, © Peter Ross
p. 107 Monticello, AFP/Getty Images
p. 108 Vartan Gregorian in front of the New York Public Library, © Sara Krulwich/*New York Times*
p. 112 Vartan Gregorian, © Rob Mayer
p. 113 Immigrants arriving at Ellis Island, © Culver Pictures, Inc.

Fearless and Free

Editor
Mary Lou Beatty

Art Director
Maria Biernik

Project Editor
Meredith Hindley

Articles Editor
Janet Wagner

Editorial Staff
Amy Lifson
Geoffrey Schramm

David Branson
Anne Fredrickson
Laura Harbold
James Kaiser
Sarah Kliff

Printed by Monarch Litho

For sale by the Superintendent of Documents, U.S. Government Printing Office
Internet: bookstore.gpo.gov   Phone: toll free (866) 512-1800;   DC area (202) 512-1800
Fax: (202) 512-2250 Mail: Stop SSOP, Washington, DC 20402-0001

ISBN 0-16-072556-9

ISBN 0-16-072556-9